HOW I LOST MY WIFE TO A WARLOCK

Learn To Thrive After Infidelity, Rebuild Your Life and Choose a Better Spouse

Trey Walters

HOW I LOST MY WIFE TO A WARLOCK. Copyright © 2023. Trey Walters. All Rights Reserved.

Printed in the United States of America.

No portion of this book may be reproduced, stored in a retrieval system, or transmitted in any form or by any means, except for brief quotations in printed reviews, without the prior written permission of DayeLight Publishers or Trey Walters.

ISBN: 978-1-958443-54-5 (paperback)

Scripture quotations marked "KJV" are taken from the Holy Bible, King James Version (Public Domain).

Scripture quotations marked (NIV) are taken from the Holy Bible, New International Version®, NIV®. Copyright © 1973, 1978, 1984 by Biblica, Inc.™ Used by permission of Zondervan. All rights reserved worldwide.

Scripture quotations marked "NKJV" are taken from the New King James Version. Copyright © 1982 by Thomas Nelson, Inc. Used by permission. All rights reserved. Bible text from the New King James Version® is not to be reproduced in copies or otherwise by any means except as permitted in writing by Thomas Nelson, Inc., Attn: Bible Rights and Permissions, P.O. Box 141000, Nashville, TN 37214-1000.

From the Author

I am the overseer of Breaking Strongholds Ministries, father of two, entrepreneur, mentor, life coach, author, and a man on a mission to advance the kingdom of heaven on earth with biblical teachings to make marriages work.

2019-2022 was the most difficult time in my life. I was drowning in debt, in and out of the hospital with one of my sons—with an illness that doctors could not diagnose—and my other son had an awful speech delay. At a very low place in life, my wife had an affair with a warlock who had one goal and that was to take us all out. The Lord favored me, and I was able to rise above it all to become a man of value.

When the Lord told me to write this book, I truly thought I was not hearing well because I never saw myself doing it. But I did it.

And we know that all things work together for good to those who love God, to those who are the called according to His purpose. (Romans 8:28 – NKJV).

Table of Contents

From the Author iii

Introduction 7

CHAPTER 1: The Beginning of the End 9

CHAPTER 2: Protocols For Marriage 13

CHAPTER 3: The Snake 19

CHAPTER 4: The Dangers of Mistreating Your Wife 23

CHAPTER 5: The Dangers of Disrespecting Your Husband 25

CHAPTER 6: Pouring Into Each Other 31

CHAPTER 7: It Takes Three to Have a Perfect Marriage 35

CHAPTER 8: Unity 39

CHAPTER 9: Know Your Enemy 43

CHAPTER 10: It Does Not Matter 45

CHAPTER 11: Money 47

CHAPTER 12: Love 55

CHAPTER 13: Delusion 61

CHAPTER 14: Life Before Christ 69

CHAPTER 15: Accepting Christ 71

CHAPTER 16: Growing in Christ 75

CHAPTER 17: Submission and Protection 79

CHAPTER 18: Choosing Destiny 83

CHAPTER 19: The Hard Choices 85
CHAPTER 20: The Betrayal 89
CHAPTER 21: Darkness Exposed 91
CHAPTER 22: Unmasking Satan 95
CHAPTER 23: Bitterness.. 97
CHAPTER 24: The Turning Point 99
CHAPTER 25: They Are After Your Children......................... 101
CHAPTER 26: Becoming the Man God Has Called Me To Be 103
CHAPTER 27: My Advice to Women....................................... 107
CHAPTER 28: My Advice For Men.. 121
CHAPTER 29: Take Control of Your Life 133
CHAPTER 30: Marriage 135
CHAPTER 31: The Snake is Now a Dragon 161
CHAPTER 32: Prayer Points 171
About the Author.. 177

Introduction

The purpose of this book is to expose the snake, not the people it manipulates, not for anyone to look down on anyone, but for everyone who reads this book to look up.

Too often, when I tell people I am writing a book about what happened, they think it is about me pointing a finger and telling the world what others did to me. Instead, I write this book to help others not make the same mistakes I, or the other individuals, made. Unfortunately, on my journey toward my destiny, I stepped in some poop. I now desire to help many see it so they don't step into it as well.

After my ordeal, I made it my mission to study where I went wrong and how my life choices led to what happened. Regardless of what happens to us in life, we will have to give an account for it. My intention was only to tell my story, but the Lord also wanted me to teach in detail how it happened and how to avoid it.

In this book, I share my story and give lessons at the same time.

CHAPTER 1

The Beginning of the End

Before getting to the how, we must understand the why, when, where, and what. Why did this happen? Where did this happen? What caused this to happen? Let me take you on a journey into the past before the words *"I do"* were uttered.

My wife grew up in a single-parent household most of her life, which is typical today. The number of children living with both parents has dropped since 1968, while the percentage living with their mother only has doubled.

In 1968, 85% of children under 18 lived with two parents (regardless of marital status); by 2020, 70% did, according to the Census Bureau's Current Population Survey (CPS).[1] So, my wife spent most of her life under a roof without her father (a typical story for most women today). The effects of this would ultimately surface in the marriage years down the line.

I grew up with both parents for a few years until I lost my father in my teens—the critical years when I needed guidance and directions on becoming a man (a typical story for the average black man). The

---

[1] https://www.census.gov/data/tables/2020/demo/families/cps-2020.html

design God established for this world to be governed correctly is for a child to be under the care and protection of both mother and father. Under different circumstances, without proper mentorship or guidance, it is evident that trouble would arise in the marriage. This is why this chapter is titled "The Beginning of the End" because there was no father in either of our households. The chances of entering a marriage with these flaws and being genuinely happy and in love are not typical. I salute the few who make it work. It is like taking off on a ship with no navigation system in place, and as the man, you should be able to lead. If you are not sure where you are going, then you are at the mercy of the wind because suddenly, you find yourself just going with the flow.

Getting married without therapy or counseling is like signing up for the Olympics without previous training or coaching. You will not get far and may not even qualify for the Olympics. There was a lot of baggage on both sides: past traumatic experiences not dealt with properly, unwillingness to change, unforgiveness, and bitterness.

This chapter is not to condemn anyone but to open the eyes of someone reading this who might be praying for a husband/wife. You need to address these issues that seem small because marriage will magnify your *"small"* problems. Marriage will expose you to yourself because no one will spend more time with you than the person you marry. For example, you can look at a man and his habits and take a wild guess where he will end up. A young man stealing, fighting, and constantly getting into trouble knows that if he doesn't change his ways, he will end up in prison or dead. Likewise, before marriage, we must analyze our habits, behavior, and patterns. Let that analysis be the compass that will guide us toward the goal of a good marriage.

If you are lustful, your marriage will not cure it but expose it under the magnifying glass we call marriage. The woman will subconsciously multiply whatever the man gives her. When a man brings his *"small"* toxic traits into the marriage, she takes it and multiplies it, creating a toxic environment. Suddenly, staying out late seems better than going home. She adds a man's bad habits to hers, and slowly that small rock will become a mountain that must be climbed daily. One begins to wonder how such a small problem can blow up into something so big. Just leaving a sock on the floor turns into a one-hour debate, and to make it worse, couples usually don't seek a marriage counselor until after the damage is done. For example, couples may seek counsel after the affair or after the physical fights. When one party is ready to get it right, the other party might not even be interested in getting it to work.

So, to whoever is reading this, pay attention to how things start because it will give an idea how it will end if no action to change is taken. As a man, you must take responsibility for everything that happens to you and around you because you will be held accountable by God. Eve ate the fruit from the tree God told them not to eat from. Nothing happened until Adam ate it as well.

So when the woman saw that the tree was good for food, that it was pleasant to the eyes, and a tree desirable to make one wise, she took of its fruit and ate. She also gave to her husband with her, and he ate. (Genesis 3:6 – NKJV).

After the act, the Lord spoke to the one who was in charge, and that was the man named Adam. Adam tried to point the finger at his wife.

> **Then the man said, "The woman whom You gave to be with me, she gave me of the tree, and I ate." (Genesis 3:12 – NKJV).**

How many men do we know who would do the same? I used to be that kind of man. I was doing this all the time in my previous marriage—*"If I had a better wife, I could be a better man,"* etc. I should have been saying, *"If I were a better man, she would have been a better wife."*

A captain must take responsibility for his ship regardless of how the crew acts. So, likewise, we must take full responsibility for our decisions and what we allow to happen. When God came to Adam for answers, he failed to take responsibility but pointed fingers at his wife. She pointed to the snake, and the snake was now ruling until Christ came, took back the power, and gave it back to us.

If you are pointing a finger at your spouse as the reason why things are going wrong, you have declared that she is now in charge. Adam was in charge at the beginning but he lost his position. Our Lord had to intervene for the story to change. If there is to be an improvement in the account you give to God, then you must be willing to allow change to find you.

CHAPTER 2

Protocols For Marriage

It is easy to say something doesn't work when we do not understand how it is supposed to work. We must take the time to understand the Blueprint; function, and purpose. We must know the role of the wife and husband. Everyone cannot be everything. Wives want to act and behave like husbands, and husbands think and work from the dimension of their wives. So many men see their mothers operating in a masculine role, which is to provide, so they grow up, get married, then find it unfair if their spouse desires to stay home. I am not saying it is a bad thing for the wife to work outside the home, but at some point in life, she will prefer being at home with the kids than dealing with work and the stress that comes with it because her natural function is to nurture.

It is hard for a woman to be in the mood when her plate has more than she can eat. If she operates outside of her feminine role, the household will be somewhat miserable, and it might cause the husband's eyes to wander elsewhere because his needs are not being met. The feminist movement of today has been one of the biggest enemies of marriage because it goes against the very structure that God gave us to go by for a blessed marriage. The same spirit that told women, *"You don't need a man,"* is the same one telling the world today, *"You don't need God."* This movement is robbing many young women and men of a fulfilling life. Most men desire a female who is loving, caring, soft, nurturing, and submissive. Still, it is hard for a woman to function in these areas if she is actively playing the role of a man.

Some women have been operating in a man's role for so long that it has become a part of their personality. It is unattractive to masculine men, so women scream, *"Where are the men?"* because the men they desire keep a safe distance from women who function like that. Kids expect their fathers to be strong, and wives want their husbands to be strong, so the man's role requires him to be strong, protect, and provide. It is the biblical blueprint God gave men to live by. The Titanic sinking years ago and sinking today wouldn't be the same because the snake has caused so much confusion in this world, fooling humanity into believing they don't need God.

And even as they did not like to retain God in their knowledge, God gave them over to a debased mind, to do those things which are not fitting; (Romans 1:28 – NKJV).

The truth will never ask us how we feel. Instead, it will challenge your false ideas of what or how you believe things should be. These are the facts: single-parent households are on the rise, and so is divorce. Over 80% of divorces filed for are by women. The snake did not leave. He is still here seeking to have dominion over us.

The protocol given is that man is the head of the house as Christ is the head of his life. The man's duty is to love his wife.

Husbands, love your wives, just as Christ also loved the church and gave Himself for her. (Ephesians 5:25 – NKJV).

The husband must be willing to die for his wife, and sometimes it is a daily thing. He must be willing to put her first and let go of pride, bitterness, etc. This is what dying to self looks like. When a man is not ready to sacrifice himself, it is best to wait before marrying and focus on self-growth.

The wife's role is submission. This is not optional. She is commanded to. She was not commanded to love but to respect her husband because the man perceives that as love.

Wives, submit to your own husbands, as to the Lord. (Ephesians 5:22 – NKJV).

I have heard women say, *"I will submit to a man if he's worth submitting to."* If you are planning to get married and this is your mentality as a woman, I suggest you inform that man that you are not yet ready for marriage and allow yourself the chance to grow in wisdom. Too many women are eager to get married just to be able to post a ring and a wedding on social media. From my previous marriage, my ex-wife was often told that because of her behavior, no man would marry her, so it was a big ego trip for her to be able to say, *"I'm married."* We can be so young and naive without a clue about what it would take for a marriage to be sustained.

Scripture tells a man the type of woman he should be searching for:

A wife of noble character who can find? She is worth far more than rubies. Her husband has full confidence in her and lacks nothing of value. She brings him good, not harm, all the days of her life. She selects wool and flax and works with eager hands. She is like the merchant ships, bringing her food from afar. She gets up while it is still night; she provides food for her family

and portions for her female servants. She considers a field and buys it; out of her earnings she plants a vineyard. She sets about her work vigorously; her arms are strong for her tasks. She sees that her trading is profitable, and her lamp does not go out at night. In her hand she holds the distaff and grasps the spindle with her fingers. She opens her arms to the poor and extends her hands to the needy. When it snows, she has no fear for her household; for all of them are clothed in scarlet. She makes coverings for her bed; she is clothed in fine linen and purple. Her husband is respected at the city gate, where he takes his seat among the elders of the land. She makes linen garments and sells them, and supplies the merchants with sashes. She is clothed with strength and dignity; she can laugh at the days to come. She speaks with wisdom, and faithful instruction is on her tongue. She watches over the affairs of her household and does not eat the bread of idleness. Her children arise and call her blessed; her husband also, and he praises her: "Many women do noble things, but you surpass them all." Charm is deceptive, and beauty is fleeting; but a woman who fears the Lord is to be praised. Honor her for all that her hands have done, and let her works bring her praise at the city gate. (Proverbs 31:10-31).

A man should be more concerned with a woman's mindset than her figure because her perspective will raise the children, and her philosophy will help the man succeed or fail. Choose wisely, and follow the protocol already set up by the Lord of lords.

Have you ever heard the phrase, *"If it ain't broke, don't fix it?"* The protocol God gave us for marriage works, and the further we stray from it, the worse things get.

Trey Walters

If my people, who are called by my name, will humble themselves and pray and seek my face and turn from their wicked ways, then I will hear from heaven, and I will forgive their sin and will heal their land. (2 Chronicles 7:14 – NIV).

CHAPTER 3

The Snake

The snake that deceived Eve is still at large, and his mission is still the same: to convince the world that the protocol God gave is of no use to us. That same snake is attacking women and is also trying to destroy the very foundation—men.

The great Roman empire fell because men's loins were out of control and burned with unquenchable lust. We see that happening today where the men of today are bound in masturbation and other sexual acts, and most of their time is spent browsing pornography websites. 2.5 million people visit the world's most popular porn sites every 60 seconds. Porn is a multi-million-dollar monster that destroys the youths of today, crippling and preventing them from being strong men of tomorrow.

Getting married will not make porn addictions go away. Some men are so dependent on porn that they cannot make love to their wives without porn being played in the same room. Lust is never satisfied and will continue pulling you into deep waters. It is a weapon of the snake to destroy men. Porn will subconsciously make a man weak if not dealt with, and just like what happened in Rome, it is happening worldwide. A woman will be friends with a weak man, but she will not marry him. If she somehow marries a weak man—

because she just wants to get married—that man's life will be hell because she will eventually be disgusted by his weakness. She will treat that man like a nobody without feeling guilty about it, so the cry of many men worldwide is, *"How could she do this to me?"* The harsh reality is that every so often, men cause this on themselves.

Behead the snake the moment you see him in your house. Reject the teaching, refuse his ideologies, and follow the protocol of the Lord. This old serpent is wise, and his goal is to produce weak men, causing them to give up their authority.

While growing up, every sitcom I saw displayed men ruled by their wives. For example, *"Everybody Loves Raymon," "George Lopez,"* etc. The snake wants to give the impression that it is normal for a man to be unhappy in a sexless marriage. But, simultaneously, his wife makes most of the decisions. So, the snake sells the phrase *"Happy wife, happy life."*

We watch men worldwide fight to make their wives happy while they die physically and spiritually. The younger men see this happening and want no part of it. The snake desires marriage to be repulsive to the younger generation. Marriage is a sacred protocol God gives us to follow and be fruitful in. We see men in leadership positions (pastors, politicians, etc.) fall under this submissive spell in secret because the serpent has been programming them from their youth.

You must protect your kids from the programming of the snake. He is after the little ones especially. He goes for the fathers so he can quickly get the kids. We also see this snake whispering in the ears of many men, causing them to be bitter and hostile toward their wives. Today they love their wives. Tomorrow they can't stand their wives; this is a breeding ground for confusion. This snake strives on chaos and confusion. This is the environment he creates to make himself more comfortable going to work.

A house divided cannot stand (see Mark 3:25), so he moves in to cause confusion, nagging, arguing, and frequent fights, and once the house is divided, he sends an agent pretending to be a knight in shining armor.

And no wonder! For Satan himself transforms himself into an angel of light. (2 Corinthians 11:14 – NKJV).

This tactical warfare must be explained before getting to the main story. When you see a motor vehicle accident, you see officers processing the scene because they want to know what led to the horrific moment. The serpent is sneaky. He will go into a house and destroy it, leaving people blaming others for whatever happened. This snake has been operating in a lot of families for years. Characters change, but the script stays the same. We see a man saying his father didn't know his father and his father didn't know his father, and it goes on until a man comes along and beheads the snake with the Sword of God.

It is wise to investigate your spouse's background before marriage because every battle they face will become your battle too, whether physically or spiritually. Not only is this snake venomous, but it can squeeze the life out of you, which is why so many husbands/wives feel suffocated and stuck. The snake will swallow you once you are broken and cannot move. This snake will cause so much distance between a couple that even though they are in the same house, they still need to shout for the other person to hear them. If he is not squeezing the life out of the marriage, his next trick is to poison it. He will bring sickness into the home—addictions/chronic illness. There are husbands/wives who want to do right, but they have a gambling addiction, alcohol addiction, porn addiction, etc. Some sicknesses and addictions develop after marriage, and many are too ashamed to seek help or they seek help when the damage is already done.

CHAPTER 4

The Dangers of Mistreating Your Wife

Husbands, love your wives and do not be bitter toward them. (Colossians 3:19 – NKJV).

I am sure we know at least one man who is guilty of mistreating his wife.

A pastor once said to me, *"Many men will be going to hell simply because of how they treat their wives."* The entire community can respect and love a husband, but if his wife is suffering under his watch, a case can be against him in heaven.

Husbands, in the same way, be considerate as you live with your wives, and treat them with respect as the weaker partner and as heirs with you of the gracious gift of life so that nothing will hinder your prayers. (1 Peter 3:7 – NIV).

The protocol is given to warn men of the danger of treating their wives harshly. In doing so, their prayers can be hindered. Men who continue to beat their wives and mistreat them in any way eventually wither away. Husband, your wife is not your equal. Don't allow the snake to bring lies into your home. If your wife considers you to be her equal, then, my friend, you are in danger, and you cannot confidently say you are the head of the house. There is a reason cars come with one steering and not two. I am not saying the wife's opinion doesn't matter. If the head is going left and the body is going right, then the neck will snap causing death. If a woman is unwilling to follow, you should go alone until you find one who sees your vision and desires to be a part of it. Avoid delusional women at all costs.

CHAPTER 5

The Dangers of Disrespecting Your Husband

Wives, respect for men equals love, so if you don't respect him, it is the same as not loving him.

The wise woman builds her house, but with her own hands the foolish one tears hers down. (Proverbs 14:1 – NIV).

There is an old adage that says, *"A woman can break you or make you; build you up or tear you down."* Wives, what you say to your husband matters. The tone in which you say it and your body language when you say it matters. It is not wise to discourage the one steering the ship even if, at the moment, he is on the wrong course. If he values your opinion, and all you do is speak ill of him, that is not wise because that means you are delaying the ship both of you are on. Sadly, many men are speaking against marriage because they are bitter about the awful experience they endured. Instead of coming out of that bad experience with wisdom on how to help other men make better choices, they come out angry and bitter. In essence, they say, *"To hell with the Blueprint God gave us. I will do this my way."*

The snake will not fight against a man who thinks like this because it is a part of his will. If it goes against the Blueprint God gave us, then it is okay with the snake because, without the blueprint, the marriage is bound to fail anyway. Wives, disrespecting your husband opens the door for him to look elsewhere for that positive encouragement he so desperately needs. If all you do is complain and insult him, then you will begin to see him less and less each day. The bars and clubs will become his new home because no man wants to fight the world and then go home to another fight. Too many women are comfortable disrespecting their husbands, and too many men have become comfortable allowing their wives to disrespect them. The more you allow disrespect, the more she continues to do it until it is big enough to knock you down in the dirt. She might not be able to beat you physically, but she can beat you emotionally, hitting you where it hurts. If the disrespect is big enough, it can leave a man homeless or in a mental hospital. It might even cost him his life.

9 WAYS YOU MIGHT BE DISRESPECTING YOUR HUSBAND

1. **You throw him under the bus in public.**

When you point out his faults, criticize or correct him in front of others, he feels like an idiot. That is demeaning. Don't embarrass him like that, especially in front of your children.

2. **You unload on him as he walks through the door.**

One thing I can't stress to wives enough—*hug* your man when he comes in from work. Greet him with a kiss and some love. Give him an encouraging word and hold off on letting him know what a rough day you had. He had a long day. You may have faced a challenging day, but show genuine love and care for your man. Take an interest in him and his day above your own. He has been hit with challenges you haven't faced, and perhaps he fought battles you will never know about. Be someone worth coming home to.

3. You expect him to be just like your girlfriends.

He is probably not a scrapbooker or a fan of spending five hours shopping. An afternoon in the nail salon is probably not his idea of fun. He is not going to communicate with you like your best friend or want to know the complete story you want to tell—down to the very last detail. Appreciate him for being a man and leave the girl stuff to your girlfriends.

4. You expect him to read your mind.

Just tell him. Don't play those mind games where you're thinking, *"If he loved me, I wouldn't have to say to him that I want him to _____."* Your husband will be so grateful if you ditch the mind-reading game and have some honest and gracious communication.

5. You treat him like your child.

Men don't think like women do, so measuring up to a woman's expectations or desires can be challenging. When a man forgets to close the lid on the toilet, it is not because he wants to irritate his wife. When a man takes the long route because he forgot the right exit, it is not because he wants to burn that extra gas. When a wife talks to her husband in the same tone she uses with her children, it is disrespectful, and that is a sin.

6. You start an emotionally-charged discussion at 11 p.m.

Don't wait until bedtime to bring up a topic of discussion that can potentially put the two of you on opposite sides of an all-out battle until near dawn. If you need to have a conversation with the potential for significant conflict or emotion, do it early in the evening (or maybe save it for the morning when he is home). Respect his need to get some rest.

7. You compare him to that "perfect guy" at church.

Your husband may not seem as *"spiritual"* as that other guy. He may not treat you the same way that *"perfect guy"* treats his wife. He may not sound as knowledgeable or seem as interested in the sermon, but your husband probably has some worthy qualities you may miss because you are so focused on what he is *"not."* Rather than comparing him to another man, why not ask God to open your eyes to see things you have not yet appreciated about him?

8. You give him the silent treatment.

Whenever you use the silent treatment to manipulate him, it harms both of you. Silent treatment is a cruel punishment tool. Don't make things more complicated by clamming up or stuffing your anger. If you are hurt or angry, ask God to search your heart to see if the anger is righteous or if some offense needs to be discussed. Talk it out with your husband. Be honest and humble in your communication, and, remember, he is not your enemy.

9. You use sex as a weapon.

The gift of sexual intimacy is an expression of unselfish love. It is a physical demonstration of spiritual unity. Don't withhold yourself to punish your husband, and don't use your intimacy as a bribe (see 1 Corinthians 7:1–5). Honor your marriage bed as sacred, and love your husband well. Put the Blueprint above your feelings.

There is a blueprint to lose weight. Still, we know people who will not follow the blueprint to lose weight because *"it is a lot of work."* Likewise, the blueprint for a successful marriage is a lot of work that not many are willing to do, yet so many talk about wanting a wife/husband.

CHAPTER 6

Pouring Into Each Other

There is a selfish generation who believes the sun rises just for them. They are not looking for someone to cultivate with, but for someone they can manipulate and control to make their lives as easy as possible.

One hand washes the other, and if your idea of marriage is *"What can you do for me?"* and not *"How can I add value to you?"* then it is a wrap. *"What do you bring to the table?"* is a question this generation constantly asks someone they desire to date, but the Blueprint shows that the man should already have this all figured out or at least have a vision.

God gave Eve to Adam to help care for what was already there. A man should seek a woman who fits the blueprint of what a good wife should be and request her to sit and eat with him in marriage. If you already have a table prepared, you will not be intimidated or concerned if she brings anything to the table except the personality the Blueprint spoke of. If she brings money and cars to the table, but her character is whack, that does nothing for the man. She should be able to pour into you in different ways as you pour into her in other ways. You will give her what she needs to feel fulfilled, and she will provide you with what you need to feel fulfilled in the marriage. However, do not wait for the other to do their part before you start doing yours.

"Well, I will start respecting him when he treats me better."

"Well, I will start treating her better when she respects me."

These statements can be likened to sitting in front of a fireplace saying, *"Give me heat, then I'll provide you with wood."* You will freeze to death with that mindset. The Bible says it is better to give than to receive. Never forget to feed the one who feeds you; pour into the one who pours into you.

The world will say otherwise, but it is on a highway to hell. Their advisor is the snake who aims to destroy them. They reject the truth because it requires change, but they accept the lie because it makes them feel justified in their wrongdoings. Men today who try to speak the truth have not taken the time to heal. They sound bitter, and it corrupts their entire message. They have not forgiven the individuals who hurt them, nor have they forgiven themselves. Instead of encouraging young men to choose better women, they encourage them not to deal with them.

This gender war is influenced by the snake because his goal remains the same after thousands of years. Sex is a part of the blueprint to get couples closer together where they can satisfy each other, so what does the snake do? He floods the market with sex toys. Married people use these devices instead of pleasuring their partner. How selfish! The device does not require pleasure, so once the user uses it and is satisfied, all is well.

We now live in an age where some husbands wait for their wives to leave the house so they can use porn to satisfy themselves; some wives are doing the same. Still, they try to justify it by saying, *"It is not cheating."* Like a drug, they are hooked and can't even stop if they want to because they have allowed the snake to pull them into a trap. With both husband and wife now pleasing themselves independently, there is little need for them to do what is needed to bring each other closer. These are selfish desires that ultimately lead to divorce.

Now for the matters you wrote about: "It is good for a man not to have sexual relations with a woman." But since sexual immorality is occurring, each man should have sexual relations with his own wife, and each woman with her own husband. The husband should fulfill his marital duty to his wife, and likewise the wife to her husband. The wife does not have authority over her own body but yields it to her husband. In the same way, the husband does not have authority over his own body but yields it to his wife. Do not deprive each other except perhaps by mutual consent and for a time, so that you may devote yourselves to prayer. Then come together again so that Satan will not tempt you because of your lack of self-control. (1 Corinthians 7:1-5 - NIV).

If you are offended by the Blueprint, I suggest you do not marry someone who lives by it.

CHAPTER 7

It Takes Three to Have a Perfect Marriage

It takes three to have the perfect marriage, according to the Blueprint: wife, husband, and the one true God make up this union. That is why the snake is doing his best to convince the world they do not need God, so for the past few years, humanity has been taking God out of schools, homes, churches, etc. We can see the negative effects of that happening all over, yet because of pride, many refuse to believe the reality of what is happening.

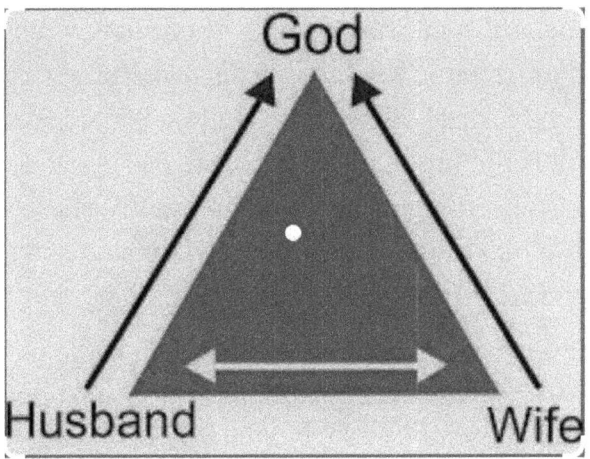

It takes God, a wife, and a husband to have a perfect marriage. Wife, husband, and religion will be a marriage of oppression. Many men of the cloth have used religion to justify their behaviors towards their wives. God is not pleased; unless they repent, it will not end well for them. If you treat everyone with respect and dignity but go home and treat your wife with disdain, God will hold you accountable. We see men respected everywhere except at home—some wives treat everyone else well but dishonor their husbands. God is needed in the center of the marriage for it to flourish.

God is the gravitational pull that keeps both husband and wife in orbit. This is why we include Him in the marital vows we take. We must remember that the Lord hates divorce (see Malachi 2:16).

But seek first his kingdom and his righteousness, and all these things will be given to you as well. (Matthew 6:33 – NIV).

A man should seek God first before seeking a wife. Too many men make the mistake of thinking they should seek wealth, then a wife, then seek God. God is full of grace and mercy, and even though you might not have married the spouse He has for you, He is willing to help you make the marriage work. Many have died in marriage because of religious individuals. A husband might be beating his wife daily, and instead of the church telling her to leave and be safe, they will ask her to return to her husband. Pastors will tell men who seek advice concerning a wife who constantly cheats to stay. It is not the will of God for His people to live in pain and sorrow. Seek God first and trust His hand to bring you the perfect spouse. Save yourself the time and pain, my friend.

Trust in the Lord with all your heart and lean not on your own understanding; in all your ways submit to him, and he will make your paths straight. (Proverbs 3:5-6 - NIV).

There are some married couples who are trying to replace God by adding an extra spouse with the hope that it can fill the void they feel.

We see couples becoming swingers, allowing someone else to sleep with their partners in their homes. Without God being involved, a marriage union will become corrupted. In these cases, there are no morals, self-respect, or respect for the spouse. God created marriage, so it is wise to sit at His feet and allow Him to teach you how to function in one.

Aim to have a perfect marriage, not an *"okay"* one. Too many people focus more on having a perfect wedding than a perfect marriage. Too many people take this serious commitment as a joke.

"It is just a piece of paper."

Well, so is money, but you still work hard to get it, and some people will do just about anything to get a lot of it. It is always tempting to complain to others about what is going wrong in a marriage because we desperately seek an outside audience to give their opinion. We often only share what the other person did wrong without seeing what we may have done to cause it.

ADDING THE WRONG PERSON IN THE TRIO

Husband: *"My wife always turns me down when I ask for sex. Like she is not interested anymore."*

Friend/Family: *"Wow, that is so selfish of her, man."*

ADDING GOD TO THE TRIO

Husband: *"My wife always turns me down when I ask for sex. Like she is not interested anymore."*

God: *"Have you been helping her around the house? She is exhausted."*

God will never be biased, and He will never lie, but we often want to hear what makes us feel good to justify ourselves. Once you bring someone else into your marriage, you set off a ticking time bomb, especially if you ask someone who doesn't know your partner like you do to advise you. God is not against therapy; some couples require it because they have refused to heed His warnings and have found themselves out of touch with His voice. He will then use a therapist to deal with the situation.

If we prepare for marriage, we will not need to repair the marriage. Wife, if you can't submit to God, how will you submit to your husband? Husband, how will you love your wife if you cannot love the Lord, your God?

CHAPTER 8

Unity

Jesus knew their thoughts and said to them, "Every kingdom divided against itself will be ruined, and every city or household divided against itself will not stand." (Matthew 12:25 – NIV).

The snake knows that a house divided cannot stand. If he can get the husband to hate his wife and the wife to hate her husband, he can get the kids. Mom and Dad are so busy with what makes them happy that they disregard their kid's happiness. If there is no unity, there is no strength.

How could one man chase a thousand, or two put ten thousand to flight, unless their Rock had sold them, unless the Lord had given them up? (Deuteronomy 32:30 - NIV).

The snake is afraid of couples who walk in agreement because that means danger for him. Unity will be established if the two agree on finances, spiritual walk, health, etc.

"Again, truly I tell you that if two of you on earth agree about anything they ask for, it will be done for them by my Father in heaven." (Matthew 18:19 – NIV).

The marriage will stagnate if the wife is constantly argumentative about everything and agrees on nothing. My advice to women is, if you will not submit to the man, then do not marry him. My advice to the man is, if she is not the type of woman to submit, then do not take her to be your wife.

2 Corinthians 6:14 instructs, **"Do not be unequally yoked together with unbelievers. For what fellowship has righteousness with lawlessness? And what communion has light with darkness?" (NKJV).**

If the situation of being unequally yoked can be avoided, it should. If someone does not believe in the standard of living that God outlines, don't tie yourself to that person. Do not fool yourself into believing it can work. Men, stop thinking with your loins. We see men complaining, *"She keeps wearing things I don't agree with."* Her reply is, *"This is what I was wearing when you met me."* It is not your job to change anyone. Don't look for someone who does not match the blueprint; it is not fair to the person.

Women complain, *"He does not want to go to church."* He replies, *"You met me on the streets."* Stop thinking you can change people and accept people for who they are. You decide if you want to stick around. Wives, if a man was a cheater before marriage, he will do the same in the union. Stop seeing the red flags and think it is a carnival.

It is hard to live in unity if the other person is not your ideal match, but if you are already married to the person, and they are willing to put in the work to make things better, then that is great. If it is not going well in your marriage, I suggest you check if there is unity. Just because there is no fighting, that does not mean there is unity.

Pay attention to who is trying to bring discord into your home. The snake loves to use others to create conflict in homes, and his secret weapon is often the in-laws.

> **"For this reason a man will leave his father and mother and be united to his wife, and the two will become one flesh." (Ephesians 5:31 - NIV).**

The Blueprint says if you have found a good wife, you should prioritize her. Too many wives are fighting for their husbands' hearts because the mom is taking up all the rooms. Am I saying you should ignore your mother? Of course not. What I am saying is, you are not married to your mother.

Too many mothers are training their sons to be their husbands. They are setting him up to fail when he seeks a wife because he will act like he has two wives. Too many fathers leave their sons to run the house and care for mom. He then grows up clinging to his mom. He ends up choosing a lousy partner and investing all his time and resources trying to be to her what his mother needed when he was growing up. He is in for a world of pain with this kind of upbringing. His job is not to go out there saving women who made terrible choices. Single mothers tend to grow their sons into the man they wish they had, which sometimes benefits them.

A mother should allow her son to be one with his wife. Too many single mothers are raising charming young men who are lousy husbands. Men, just because you saw Mom doing it alone doesn't mean you should let your wife do the same. Follow the Blueprint from start to finish. Do more than just take out the parts that sound good to you.

If you try to use these principles on someone the Blueprint warns you not to marry, you will suffer greatly. Submit fully to the Blueprint, resist the teaching of this world, and the snake will leave.

Submit yourselves, then, to God. Resist the devil, and he will flee from you. (James 4:7 – NIV).

CHAPTER 9

Know Your Enemy

Marriage is a battlefield, and you must know your enemy; don't be your own enemy. In marriage, the two become one. If you fight against your spouse, you are at war with yourself. Divide and conquer has always been a weapon of the snake. If it can get a house to turn on itself, it can watch them fall from the outside. We see great nations on the brink of collapse because they are divided, while the real criminals profit from their ignorance.

Years ago, four men robbed a bank and stole four million dollars, but the bank gave a different report. The bank stated that ten million dollars was stolen. This caused a division between the four men as they all started to suspect each other of holding out. One man killed the other three men and was later caught and arrested. The bank baited the men into seeing each other as the enemy.

Choosing a partner who believes in the Blueprint and lives by it is essential because this person will also have integrity and do the right thing, even when no one is looking. Regardless of what is going on, a person of integrity will stand on the value of the Blueprint and not defile themselves with the opinions of the snake.

China built the Great Wall to keep its enemies out, but China was invaded three times without a single man coming over that wall because the gatekeeper was bribed, and they let the enemy in. Men, don't allow strange women to bribe you with sex to let them into your marriage to destroy it. Do not be enticed by what is being offered that you let the enemy into your home. Wives, do not be bribed with a bit of excitement by strange men that you allow them into your marital bed to defile it and rip your house apart. An enemy of your spouse is also your enemy. Anything that puts your family at risk is your enemy, and you need to be able to recognize this.

Also, to know your enemy, you must know yourself; study hard because the snake studies you. Many men have fallen because they failed to acknowledge their weaknesses until they find themselves alone with a beautiful woman. If they had acknowledged their weaknesses, they would have a rule to never be alone in a room with the opposite sex. Don't become the weapon formed against yourself. Become a no-nonsense person who will not smile at the enemy because he is not smiling at you. He will destroy you, if given a chance, and the more room you give him, the more space he will demand until he moves from tenant to landlord, and you find yourself fighting for a spot in your own home.

Be alert and of sober mind. Your enemy the devil prowls around like a roaring lion looking for someone to devour. (1 Peter 5:8 - NIV).

CHAPTER 10

It Does Not Matter

How you feel about a situation won't change the facts. It is vital that you put feelings aside so you can grow. It does not matter who you are or where you came from. What matters is that you adapt to the Blueprint given and stick to it.

One day, a man was driving, and he turned onto a road that had recently turned into a one-way. A police officer saw him and pulled him over. The man started to explain to the officer that he had no idea he was breaking the law, but the officer pulled out his ticket book and said, *"It doesn't matter."*

"What do you mean?" the man asked.

The officer said, *"Ignorance is not an excuse to break the law."*

If you follow the Blueprint or not, these laws will still stand, and many people will choose to learn the hard way. Growing up without a father is sad, but it is not a free pass to live as a weak or confused man for the rest of your life. A woman is looking for a man, not a boy she has to show how to be a man. It does not matter what your reason for falling short is. Likewise, a man is looking for a woman; he doesn't want to be constantly reminding her how to treat him.

No matter how good your excuses are, it does not matter, especially if you are a man.

Standing before a judge for not having a father-figure will not reduce your crime sentence. Life is like a fertile land. The land does not care what you plant, but you will reap what you sow. It does not matter if you drink poison by accident or not; the effects will be the same. If you work against the Blueprint, the results will be the same.

The suicide rate among men keeps rising. Regardless of nationality or background, men are dying at an alarming rate, and many for the same reason. Too often emotions push logic through the door, and we forget what is and try to highlight what could, should or would have been. I am a fan of the Judge Judy show, and every so often she would say, *"It doesn't matter."* What she wants to see is evidence to prove if what is being said is true. There are too many in this *"entitled"* generation who believe the world should pause for them.

CHAPTER 11

Money

Finances is listed as the second leading cause of divorce globally; yet people act as if money doesn't matter. Love will not pay the bills. There is no nobility in poverty. Yes, many lessons come from being poor, but one should never get comfortable being poor. A man who cannot provide for his family faces sleepless nights. It brings great joy when a man can tell his family, *"Don't worry. I got this."* Money is good when in the hands of a disciplined man, and the Blueprint speaks of this. Too many men in this generation want to make easy or fast money, which goes against the Blueprint. Prison is full of people who thought easy and quick money would keep them happy.

Dishonest money dwindles away, but whoever gathers money little by little makes it grow. (Proverbs 13:11 – NIV).

This is where the character of a person is built. The man who gains money in this manner is a respectable man who lives by a code of honor and loyalty. Those in the fast lane would sacrifice their own family for the riches of this world. The LOVE of money is the root of all evil, not money itself. Money is a tool for the wise.

> **Such are the paths of all who go after ill-gotten gain; it takes away the life of those who get it. (Proverbs 1:19 – NIV).**

I have seen many young men in my community "die trying" while seeking to get rich in the fast lane. I live in Jamaica, where most of the bloodshed across the island is caused by scamming. Scammers are people who rob the elderly and vulnerable, then turn around and kill each other for the profits made from their ill-gotten gains. Those not killed are locked away from their family for years.

MONEY WILL MAGNIFY WHOEVER YOU ARE

If you are an adulterer at heart, you will commit adultery. Many men think they are not adulterers, but that is because they have no money to act on it. The Blueprint states that lusting after a woman in your heart makes you guilty of adultery. A man is tested when he has money. A man does not make money and then suddenly becomes prideful. Pride has always been in him; now he is acting it out.

So many men have decided that the woman who has been by their side through thick and thin is no longer the woman for them because they now have money. Too many women have turned around and kicked the man who loves them to the curve because they make more money than him. Too many women are screaming, *"I don't need a man because I make six figures."* Money in the hands of an emotional and undisciplined person will be their downfall. This is a familiar story for many.

> **The rich rule over the poor, and the borrower is slave to the lender. (Proverbs 22:7 – NIV).**

Too many couples are drowning in debt. Focusing on your spouse is hard when you are busy wondering if the bank is coming to take the car or house away. Years ago, we did not need a lot of material things to be comfortable. Heat, water, and shelter were enough for many, but this generation wants Wi-fi, cars, Louis Vuitton bags, high-tech electronics, and the list continues to grow yearly. Being deep in debt but eating out every night is now a common practice for many couples. Sooner or later, petty arguments over money will arise because wherever there is a lack of money, there is a lack of surety.

"Honey, are we getting this for Timmy?"

"Honey, are we taking the kids to the beach?"

"Honey, are we keeping a party for the kids next month?"

"Honey, are we going out this weekend?"

The answer to all these questions is *"I'm not sure."*

Telling a woman, *"I'll see what I can do,"* often breaks her trust and lowers her dependency on you to come through for her. When you find yourself in a pit, it is best to stop digging and figure out how to escape it.

Do not be one who shakes hands in pledge or puts up security for debts; if you lack the means to pay, your very bed will be snatched from under you. (Proverbs 22:26-27 – NIV).

Debts should be approached with extreme caution. In our modern society, debt is far too easy to accumulate. The economic system provides for this ease. Student loans, mortgages, and credit cards abound. Beyond the fact that debt puts us in bondage, consumer debt makes it extremely difficult to build wealth.

Seek to pay off your credit card debt if you are in it, and then once you get all your consumer debts paid off, it is time to focus on paying off the mortgage early. **Follow the Blueprint and protect your family.**

THE LOVE OF MONEY

According to the Blueprint, the love of money is the root of all evil. In 2006, a man named Abraham Shakespeare won a $31 million jackpot and did not live to spend it. His financial advisor, Dorice Moore, took advantage of her client's inability to read and write well. She spent that man's money on herself and her lover. A few weeks later, he went missing, and his body was found buried under a concrete slab at one of his financial advisor's houses.

The love of money will make people do unimaginable things. The great author of the Blueprint was sold out for thirty pieces of silver. That should be enough to show you how dark a man's heart can become when money becomes his god. We should love God and use money, but many love money and use God. *"God, if You let me get this, I promise to serve You."* After getting that very thing, they forget about God until they find themselves in another pit.

The wealth of the rich is their fortified city; they imagine it a wall too high to scale. (Proverbs 18:11 – NIV).

Money is a wall of defense for your family. Money keeps the heat going in the house during winter. Money keeps food on the table and keeps you from being homeless. Let it be your tool for having a decent life. Once you see it as just a tool to get a job done, it prevents you from falling into the trap of greed that devours so many.

"Let the Lord be magnified, Who has pleasure in the prosperity of His servant." (Psalms 35:27b – NKJV).

God wants you to have money. He wants you to prosper. He wants you to be able to take care of your family, and He wants you to have a happy life and a fruitful marriage. Don't promise a woman the world at the altar without knowing how to get her the simple things in life. Don't buy into the delusion that making a woman happy does not take much. Become a man of value and invest in yourself. The more value you add to yourself, the higher the quality of life you can provide for your family.

MONEY ALONE WON'T CUT IT

Money alone won't make your home function properly. It is a well-needed tool, but that alone won't make it function properly. The engine is significant in a vehicle, but it is not the only equipment that makes it move. There are many men who believe having a lot of money would make their marriage work, but time has proven them wrong. Some of the wealthiest men alive are divorced or currently going through a divorce. Most of these divorces are being filed by the wives. Handsome, rich men are being handed divorce papers worldwide.

Statistics show that many marriages end because of money problems. Money alone won't keep your marriage going or these wealthy men would still be married today. The Blueprint is a code no man can push aside and believe he is above it. An airplane is built to go above the law of gravity, but for how long? Eventually, it must come down. For ten years, you might have been able to ignore this Blueprint and barely keep your marriage afloat by doing strange things to keep it going, but eventually, it will fall, screaming, *"May day. May day. My marriage is falling."* Many marriages are screaming for help today because the couples are not doing what the Blueprint says. Work on your soul as much as you work on your finances because out of the abundance of the heart the mouth speaks. When you see men with money choosing wives with the characteristics of a Jezebel/Delilah, inevitably, he will quickly realize that being alone in the wilderness is better than being in a mansion with that woman.

Better to live on a corner of the roof than share a house with a quarrelsome wife. (Proverbs 21:9 – NIV).

Better to live in a desert than with a quarrelsome and nagging wife. (Proverbs 21:19 – NIV).

Some women seek men to ensnare them in their web of manipulation so they can drain them financially and emotionally. They do not respect or care for these men, and these men are blinded by the women's beauty and shape, failing to see the spell cast over their minds. These women usually manipulate weak men to:

- stay away from their biological kids.
- not allow their family to come around much.
- only value her side of the family.
- give her everything.

The man's health/happiness means nothing to her. She breaks him down, then takes half of his wealth, all while playing the victim. Very few men find their way back after encountering this type of woman. Some commit suicide, some are killed, while others struggle to recover mentally and financially.

Alishia Noel-Murray was found guilty of murder after hiring a hitman to kill her husband to claim the US$900,000 life insurance. Linda Calvey was known as the black widow. All her lovers ended up dead or in prison. After six months of marriage, the beautiful Evelyn Dick removed her husband's head and left his body in the woods. Mary Wilson married four times and killed all four of her husbands, earning her the nickname *"Merry Widow of Windy Nook."* This happened so often that people have started TV series and documentaries on these events, and there is always new material for continuing new episodes.

A woman can build or destroy a man. A man should never underestimate a woman. An entire army could not defeat Samson, but it took one woman to bring him down, which is happening to this day.

While writing this, I heard a report of a young man who was shot and killed by an off-duty police officer after he tried to discourage his girl from going into the car of the off-duty cop. Though the young man was unarmed, the policeman still shot him dead. His love and affection for this woman resulted in him losing his life; a fate that could have easily been mine without God's grace, but I will get to that chapter soon.

This is not just about telling my story but allowing my God to use me to help others not to make the same mistakes I made.

CHAPTER 12

Love

We are in the last days. The Blueprint warns us that many would become lovers of themselves. This generation is an *"It's all about me"* generation. Too many people believe the world revolves around them, and that mindset will hurt any relationship.

Today, men and women get married and still want to act single because it is seen as *"self-love."*

"Girl, don't let that man stop you from living your best life."

"Do you, girl."

"Bro, forget her. Go get a girl on the side that makes you feel good."

Everyone wants to do what makes them feel good, but this is not real love. According to the Blueprint, many will mistake selfishness for love in this age. The Blueprint tells us what love is.

Love is patient, love is kind. It does not envy, it does not boast, it is not proud. It does not dishonor others, it is not self-seeking,

it is not easily angered, and it keeps no record of wrongs. (1 Corinthians 13:4-5 – NIV).

Pause and reflect on this scripture. Does this describe your relationship?

LOVE IS PATIENT

Are you patient with your spouse? Do you give him/her room to grow or adapt to living with you?

So many have missed out on good relationships because they were impatient.

LOVE IS KIND

Being kind and being nice is not the same thing. Young men and women are finding this out the hard way. A *"nice"* person is not really respected, but a generous man is. The *"kind"* man will not tolerate disrespect and will not give up his peace on the inside to keep peace on the outside. Often nice people will allow losing their peace on the inside to keep peace on the outside. Too often, that leads to them being taken advantage of. Being *"nice"* is not something a woman finds attractive, so we continue to hear, *"Nice guys finish last."* Be kind to everyone, especially your spouse.

LOVE IS NOT ENVIOUS

Too many people are jealous of their spouse.

Anger is cruel and fury overwhelming, but who can stand before jealousy? (Proverbs 27:4 – NIV).

There is no telling what you would do to your partner once envy creeps in. You would eventually resent your partner and then find ways to sabotage their growth. Celebrate your spouse and be happy for them.

LOVE DOES NOT BOAST

Your partner doesn't want you to constantly remind them of what you did for them.

"If it was not for me…"

Even if they appreciate what you did, if you are boastful, they will be sorry they allowed you to help them. Eventually, they will desire to do everything on their own, even if that means struggling to do so. You do not want your partner to get to that place.

LOVE DOES NOT DISHONOR

Dishonoring your spouse is not love or *"tough love."* So many people embarrass their spouses on purpose and think it is funny.

"I just wanted him/her to feel a little jealous."

If your spouse gives someone else a reason to laugh at you or look down at you, wake up and understand that that is not love. Suppose he/she is making you look bad in the eyes of others in any shape or form; that is not love.

LOVE IS NOT SELF SEEKING

Making decisions that will only benefit you is selfish. For example, if it is your spouse's birthday, but instead of taking your spouse somewhere they want to go, you go somewhere you always wanted to go and try to convince your spouse it is better to go to that place because you like it; that is selfish. Being selfish is always making things about you and your feelings and not being concerned about the other person.

LOVE IS SLOW TO ANGER

It feels like walking on eggshells when dealing with someone who is quick to anger. It is very hard to communicate with such a person because it normally leads to an argument.

LOVE KEEPS NO RECORD OF WRONG DOING

Forgive and forget. Your spouse will make errors and won't get everything right, and the last thing they want is to constantly be reminded of what they did wrong. Too many people talk about what was done to them twenty years ago. When a person is trying their best to be better, it is discouraging when you bring up the past. Why argue over a situation that was already acknowledged and discussed?

LEADING IN LOVE

Before you try to lead anyone, ask yourself, *"Do I love this person?" "Does this person know I love them?"* The challenge many husbands face is getting their wives to follow them.

Women are emotional, and it is hard to get them to let your goal become theirs if they do not feel loved. So many men are unsure how to express their feelings, and this causes a frustrating cycle. She desires to feel loved, and the man loves her but does not know how to communicate his love in a language she understands. Some men don't even love themselves. If you do not love yourself, you won't be able to love a woman properly. If you cannot love her properly, she won't respect you. If she doesn't respect you, she won't follow you, no matter how solid your plan is.

She won't care how much you know until she knows you care, and that is a natural response from a woman because it is her nature. If you never tell your blood brother you love him, he knows you do, but a woman will constantly ask if you love her. Even if you donated one of your kidneys to her, she will still ask if you love her. That is her nature. Husband, if you don't know how to love, you are not ready to lead, and a woman desires a man who knows how to lead.

Learn to love yourself, heal from childhood traumas, and know where you are going in life. Let the Lord be your source for all things.

CHAPTER 13

Delusion

In this age, people are under a strong delusion because they have rejected the Blueprint. Many stand in high places, ripping the Blueprint apart for the world to see.

And for this cause God shall send them strong delusion, that they should believe a lie: (2 Thessalonians 2:11 – KJV).

The delusion is so strong that many cannot tell their right hand from their left. Social media is filled with people who have platforms that share their delusions with the younger generation.

DELUSIONAL MEN

Some men believe they deserve the Proverbs 31 woman, while they refuse to become the man a Proverbs 31 woman wants. They want a woman who is a virgin and is good in bed. They want a woman who will put up with their destructive habits and disrespect. They think a woman should love them, whether they bring value or not. They want women to accept them as they are and be happy about that. They think a woman should bring her half to the table and support them financially. She should be loyal in the marriage but not accept loyalty. These delusional teachings are accepted from bitter men on massive platforms who have not healed from past hurt; they resent women. The intentions may be good but cause more harm than good.

You can be killed if someone loves you dearly and accidentally puts poison in your water. A few men with good intentions, who have suffered at the hands of their ex-spouse, try to help other men not go through what they did, but they try to help from a place of hurt. Don't buy the unicorn meat being sold that as a man, you should be more feminine and open up to your spouse about your struggles and dark past. This looks good on paper but is useless in reality. Seek out a professional therapist if you feel your burden is too much.

I am not saying you should not communicate with your spouse, and you shouldn't let her know how you are feeling. But don't sit there crying your eyes out about life. Be a strong man in the eyes of your family at all times.

Women in this generation encourage men to be more open, but they don't want to be with them. Men will tell you it is not a good idea to show your broken side to your spouse. It is often thrown back in their faces at later dates. *"Should, would, could"* are not essential, but the fact of *"What is."*

"Women <u>should</u> not use a man's pain against him."

"I don't think my spouse <u>would</u> use it against me."

"I don't think my spouse <u>could</u> use it against me."

The fact is, there is a strong possibility she will. She might be sorry and apologize for it, but the damage will already be done to your self-esteem. Avoid that path and learn from men who have already passed that stage.

DELUSIONAL WOMEN

The feminist movement of today has eaten the bread of sorrow and is regurgitating nonsense. Feelings and emotions back their ideas that goes against every order of the Blueprint, and sadly, it is at an old age that most of these women wake up and see the errors they accepted as normal.

It is a delusion for a woman to think you can sleep around with as many men as you want, and when you are ready to find the man of your dreams—usually an above-average man—he should accept you with open arms and put a ring on your finger because your past shouldn't matter. Women like to hear about a man's future because they want to know where he is going. If he was dead-broke last year, but this year he seems to be going places, it doesn't matter. More questions are asked concerning his future than his past.

At the same time, a man is more concerned about a woman's past and upbringing. As a woman, you are born with value. In the old days, when villages were conquered by their enemies, they would kill the men and boys but leave the women and girls to cultivate. But the snake system teaches you to devalue yourself, so you agree with the idea that it doesn't matter how you live your life.

There is a delusion that the husband is not the head. Can two heads on a body make it function properly? How many steering wheels are in a vehicle? Do you want a man you consider your equal to be your husband? Would you be attracted to such a man? Would you respect him? Would that man be able to protect you? The idea that you shouldn't listen to your husband but go to work and listen to your boss sounds strange and delusional. It is a delusion to think that the more money you make, the more attractive you become to the man you desire. Having ambition and working hard to get your finances in order is great, but it doesn't matter to a man because he knows his money ends up being *"our"* money, but your money will always be yours.

Studies show that the more a woman climbs the corporate ladder, the less desirable she becomes. Men don't find you less desirable because you earn a lot of money, but the attitude that comes with that turns men off. Women have divorced their husbands because of their promotion at work. They feel that now, because they earn more, they can, for some reason, treat the man like a child, and they often leave the marriage to seek a more established man. I have seen men invest resources in their women to take them to higher heights, and the woman turns around and starts looking at that man as if he is now below her. Thankfully, not all women are like that.

Having a preference is okay, but don't make it an idol. If you think because he is not a 6-foot-tall billionaire, he is not the one for you, do you actually believe a 6-foot-tall billionaire is looking for you? If you did happen to date one, what are the chances he would get down on one knee and ask you to marry him? Don't believe that because a man is interested in dating you, he is interested in marrying you. It is good to have an idea of the man you want, but it will end badly if that becomes an idol in your heart. Find out what is available in the dating market, and stop wishing on stars for a man who doesn't exist.

DO NOT PARTNER WITH DELUSIONAL PEOPLE

If you attach yourself to someone delusional, it will not end well. Imagine starting a business with someone who, instead of going with the facts on how to create a successful business, chooses to follow the feelings and opinions of people who are not successful business owners. Marriage can be seen as a business; hence, the signing of contracts, and not many people will honor the contract they signed. They neglect their obligations to protect, provide, and nurture in good times and bad.

I once heard a successful businessman state that he would not do business with a man who cheats on his wife, and his reasons for that is, if a man is willing to run the risk of destroying his own home and losing his family for pleasure, then he cannot be trusted to honor his word concerning business. What would stop that man from betraying him in business?

If a woman believes she can be the head of the house alongside the man, why would she submit after marrying? If the man believes he should have more than one woman, why would you believe after marrying him that he would be loyal to you? The snake is counting on us to make this mistake so he can delay or destroy our assignment.

If you marry someone who doesn't believe that witchcraft, sorcery, and other weapons of the snake are real, then guess who will be fighting these things alone? You can do your best to show them the snake, but if they keep denying or believing that there is a snake, they will not understand what you do. When people don't understand something, they reject, mock, then hate it. After a while, they hate your prayer life and might even hate you for it.

Be ye not unequally yoked together with unbelievers: for what fellowship hath righteousness with unrighteousness? and what communion hath light with darkness? And what concord hath Christ with Belial? Or what part hath he that believeth with an infidel? (2 Corinthians 6:14-15 – KJV).

This does not mean these people are bad. Tying yourself to them would not be wise because it would hinder or destroy your life. Men should try not to be persuaded by looks.

Do not lust after her beauty in your heart, nor let her allure you with her eyelids. For by means of a harlot a man is reduced to a crust of bread; And an adulteress will prey upon his precious life. (Proverbs 6:25-26 – NKJV).

You have been warned! If you fall for these types of women, your suffering has just started.

Stumble not at the beauty of a woman, and desire her not for pleasure. (Sirach 25:21 - KJV).

Do not fall for her just because she looks good and you desire her body.

[Give me] any plague, but the plague of the heart: and any wickedness, but the wickedness of a woman: (Sirach 25:13 - KJV).

I know a man who went abroad and financially supported a woman living on the island for years. He thought that when he came back home, he was coming to a wife and a house. When he got back, he saw no house and the woman had another man. She had no remorse about it. His recovery was a long, painful one.

Hell has no fury like a woman scorn. Entangle yourself with a broken, angry woman, and you will feel wrath like never before.

I had rather dwell with a lion and a dragon, than to keep house with a wicked woman. (Sirach 25:16 - KJV).

I have seen men whose wives got pregnant for someone—friend or enemy—they know very well. These are the kinds of wickedness that can make you mentally unstable.

This is the way of an adulterous woman: She eats and wipes her mouth and says, 'I've done nothing wrong.' (Proverbs 30:20 – NIV).

After destroying your life, this kind of woman will not feel bad about doing it. She will live her life like nothing happened while you scramble to find hope.

Women should endeavour not to be persuaded by lies.

Let no one deceive you with empty words, for because of such things God's wrath comes on those who are disobedient. (Ephesians 5:6 – NIV).

It is a lot easier to get a woman by lying to her and pretending to be someone you are not.

CHAPTER 14

Life Before Christ

Before I came to Christ, I was that young man who was focused on sex and how to get a lot of it. I didn't know that that mentality was the most effective time-wasting strategy the snake puts before men. The time and effort men put into chasing women is a big distraction to pull them from destiny and defile them simultaneously. Sex was designed for husband and wife.

Unfortunately, we have a people cluelessly walking around with a spirit-spouse. A spirit-spouse is a spirit that attaches itself to someone through sexual immorality, and it will have sex with that person via dreams, and consume that person with lust. As more people engage with this spirit, society becomes more consumed by lust, and a generation full of lust will not make good husbands/wives.

I was a drifter, just going with the flow of life. There was no definite aim or goal. This is a sad path that too many young men find themselves on. Eventually, I got to where I wanted to experience life with someone on a broader scale. If, at the time, I had already been in the body of Christ, the story would have turned out differently. I had no mentor, long-term goal, structure, wisdom, discipline, or idea about the Blueprint—the Holy Bible. John C.

Maxwell, the leadership expert, gets all his teaching material from this book, which says a lot.

I met another drifter and decided to get married. It didn't take long for things to start going downhill because it was a learning process. I took the test without studying, so everything was done with the hope that something positive would come out of it. There were a lot of trials and errors, and each mistake was like a brick being placed between us. Finances were in shambles with a pit that kept getting deeper and wider with each error. At this point, I was starting to doubt the existence of God even more, and the part of me that believed He was real was blaming Him for every negative thing that was happening to me because I was trying to live a life I believed was a noble one.

CHAPTER 15

Accepting Christ

I accepted Christ after someone close to me died. It was not that person's death alone that had me seeking God but what happened after. After hearing that he committed suicide, one look at his body, and you could see evidence of foul play. A family member asked me then if I wanted to know the truth. She knew a lady who could give me the answers I sought. I was hurting and needed answers, so I agreed to see the lady. That started a chain of circumstances that would lead up to today.

A family member and I went to this place, and when I got there, I was surprised to see the long line in the waiting area. I saw a table with candles, grapefruit, herbs, a bason with water, and a few small statues. I looked around, trying to understand what this was all about and why the people were hopeful. I started to feel uncomfortable with the beating of the drums and everything happening around me. It felt like time began to move in slow motion, and then it was our time to go into the room to speak to the woman.

The woman sitting down in the room surrounded by candles started to talk. She said my family member did not commit suicide, but he was beaten to death. Someone used a blunt object to the head, and it was later proven so by the autopsy. She told us of the men who committed this brutal act. She then asked, *"Who is Shane?"* Only close family members called me by that name. I was concerned but unconvinced. She then called me by a name only my father called me at home, and that was when she had my full attention. She said, *"The angel said they are after you. They want to kill you too."*

I asked, *"Who wants to kill me and why?"*

She answered, *"The same ones who killed your family member."*

I said, *"I don't know these men, so why would I be a target."*

She said, *"Because, like your family member, you are set apart to be great with house and cars, and they want to snatch you away before it happens. These spirits are hunting you."*

My knees got weak. For weeks, I kept dreaming of men chasing me and shooting at me. I could not deny or explain anything that happened that day, but I knew the spiritual realm was real. She told me to come back to see if she could help me. She didn't need to convince me to come back to see her. She gave me four candles and a scripture to read, but I had many questions. Having the scriptures with the candles made it easier to work with. She told me to take the candles home and place them in the four corners of the room. If I knew the Word of God, I would have known from the beginning that this was not of God. This act only gave me a sense of false peace and safety.

After doing that, every 6 o'clock, I would feel a strange presence enter the house. I remember sitting on the bed, and not only did I feel this presence in the room, but I saw the bed sink as if someone had just sat down. I remember running out of the house that day, confused and angry because I did not know how to fight whatever came into my home.

A few days later, I was watching a movie with the children's mother. I saw her looking at the door with her eyes wide open, but she could not speak. Then she passed out. When she woke up, she said a lady came through the door and entered her. I didn't know what to do, so I went back to the lady for help. She gave me some herbs to burn in the house. I was provoked to start seeking the face of the God I heard about growing up, but I still visited the lady a few more times. I was also frustrated with the church system because I saw no power. Eventually, I started studying the Word of God and watching YouTube videos about the spirit realm. I gave my life to Christ gladly.

The evidence was too clear to ignore. If the forces of darkness are real, then the forces of light must be real, and the Bible must be true because it speaks of all the things I experienced that could not be explained outside of that Blueprint. Consulting these *"other"* people is dangerous; the Blueprint warns against seeing them. They do far more harm than good and take far more than they give. The lack of knowledge of the consequences of seeking mediums is destroying people. After about a year of that experience, I gave my life to God and accepted Jesus Christ as my Lord and Savior.

CHAPTER 16

Growing in Christ

After accepting Christ, you must decide how far you want to go in Christ. After being exposed to real-life witches, I wanted to know as much as possible. The typical religious lifestyle was not for me. I wanted to know King Jesus for myself.

At this point, I started to strive to make changes in a marriage that was already damaged, and I was confident the Lord wanted to restore the marriage, but the seed of unforgiveness was planted in my children's mother. I made errors along the way, and they watered that seed of unforgiveness. As time passed by, it became more challenging to have a conversation with her.

Though I was growing in Christ, I still had feeble leadership and communication skills. I was sometimes matching her energy when I should have been leading by example. *"If you do not want to talk, then I won't talk either"* was the mindset most of the time. After a while, I got tired of explaining the warfare and decided to fight it alone. When a woman has a mental picture of who you are in her head, it is not easy to undo, and she has the ability to lose every drop of feelings for you but still stay around even though mentally she has already left you.

THE POWER OF A WOMAN IN MARRIAGE

The Blueprint shows us that God gave Satan the green light to afflict Job. Satan did many things to Job—killing his children and livelihood—but never touched his wife. He didn't forget to kill her. Satan knew she would be of better use to him alive. A man can stand firm against the entire world, but a home without peace is a battle he can only withstand for so long. Job's wife told him to curse God and die. Luckily, Job, being wise, told her she was a foolish woman just for saying that.

Having a spouse who doesn't believe in you or discourages you is another psychological warfare that has hindered or caused many people to give up or settle. This is Satan weaponizing the person God designed to be a blessing in your life. If Christ is not the head of your life, you will be broken in every way if Satan uses your wife against you. So many men have become homeless, useless, etc., because, at some point, their wives became their enemies. When you have an enemy at home, you find yourself in bars and other dark places. Mentally, I was in a bad place, but I was still trying to go forth toward the promises. Whenever a breakthrough came my way, the enemy would use her to stir up anger and rage in me, and I would miss the breakthrough.

In the earlier chapters, I went into detail about the consequences of being at war with your spouse, and this cycle went on for at least three years. When the enemy realized romance was completely gone from the marriage, he formulated a trap to destroy me. Sexual traps are the most frequent tool used by the enemy against men of God—old or young.

OVERCOMING THE SEXUAL AGENTS OF DARKNESS

One day, a man of God told me that he saw, in a vision, the enemy sending a woman to eradicate the marriage and bring me down. He told me the shoe size this woman wore, her height, and her complexion. A woman fitting this role did walk into my life, and like a fool, I convinced myself that this woman must not be the one he talked about because she was very friendly and seemed okay. We became friends, and she would encourage me, so we got closer every day.

One day, she invited me out. I didn't like being home anyway, so I agreed to go, but I felt in my spirit that I shouldn't go. I convinced myself that I had on the whole armor of God and I would be okay. I went with this young lady to the beach. Everything was okay until we went into the water together. The waves were a bit rough, and I held her in my arms. Things escalated quickly, and so many thoughts ran through my mind. Blood was rushing from my brain to other parts of my body. I could feel the sun on my skin and hear the seagulls flying overhead as the waves crashed into our bodies. Time was moving very slowly, and when she felt what was being pressed against her, she told me she was down for whatever, and her body was mine to take if I wanted. Already wet and sweating, I had to ask God to deliver me from this encounter because I could not walk away on my own.

With each passing second, I felt myself drifting to react to the needs of my flesh. Then, it felt like a door was opened. Some children playing a ball game nearby threw a ball right beside me, and hearing that ball hit the water woke me out of what felt like a trance. I let her go and told her I was ready to leave.

A few days later, she got so sick she thought she would die. That was when I started to step back until all connections were broken. That was one of many traps the enemy threw at me as I continued to grow in the things of God.

CHAPTER 17

Submission and Protection

As I continued to grow in my walk, the attacks became more extensive, and my poor leadership in the past came back to haunt me. As the warfare increased, I would try to warn the children's mother to stay alert, but my words seemed to have fallen on deaf ears. Nothing I said was taken seriously.

I woke up in the night seeing spirits in the house, and after I rebuked them, I wondered how and what door they were entering through. The truth is, there were many open doors. It doesn't matter how righteous you try to live, if both sides are not living a virtuous life, that gives the enemy access to the home. Husband, if your wife is not submitted to you, you cannot protect her. Sadly, looking out for your spouse's protection today is seen as toxic. A man will see people trying to harm his woman long before she notices what is happening. He would point out the red flags. If the woman does not submit to him and acknowledge him as the head, then she will ignore his warnings. This was the scenario I was in.

I had failed to take her along the journey I was on and failed in so many other areas in the early stages. She refused my hand in leadership, so I was at war all around. She would go to places with her friends and come back with demons that I would have to deal with, and the burden was getting too much. A man must protect, and I was failing miserably at this. It didn't matter how peaceful I tried to live, the house always felt like a battlefield because it was now at a point where she hated me for trying to "control her." Someone else was in her ears, and time would reveal who that was.

"Not everybody that you fight is your enemy, and not everybody who helps you is your friend." —Tyson

This is a lesson she would soon find out.

A servant of God came with a word from the Lord: *"Get your house in order."*

I remember feeling so frustrated at that point. I just couldn't understand why she wouldn't believe me. If God spoke directly to her, she might finally see the truth. I soon realized that the Lord is all about order. He always speaks to the one in charge and expects them to address issues within their home, ministry, etc. So, despite my frustration, I knew the Lord was speaking to me about matters concerning her for a reason.

As a believer, I have come to realize that pastors, evangelists, and other men of God are at risk of missing out on heaven due to the lack of order in their homes. As the head of the household, the Lord will hold you accountable for your wife's conduct. It is crucial to ensure that your household is in order and aligned with God's Word to avoid repercussions.

I told my wife that she was married to a wanted man. The forces of darkness were coming after me, and if she did not wake up to reality, she would see what I had been trying to tell her for years.

The battle was intense. The people of God kept praying that I would not die, but no one was telling me what was going on.

CHAPTER 18

Choosing Destiny

"I ignored my destiny once; I cannot do that again, even for you."

—Thanos

I vividly recall when I was in a severe battle for my destiny. I cried out to the Lord, begging for protection and guidance to stay on the path meant for me. It was difficult, and I knew I might miss out on my calling without divine intervention.

One night, I encountered a frightening spirit that entered my home. It held a knife made of bone, and the spirit had strange markings on its body. The spirit claimed that I was not righteous and deserved to die. I immediately spoke up, proclaiming that it wasn't my own works that made me righteous but my faith in Jesus Christ. The spirit left, and I knew it was a sign of God's protection and love for me.

After a few days, I started to have very sharp pains in my chest, and I would have dreams of collapsing and holding my chest. My family in Christ kept praying for me that I would live and that the warlock would not prevail. I would listen to the prayers and try to put the pieces together. I knew a warlock was attempting to take me out, but I was unsure who, where, and what. I felt tormented. I could not function correctly, and, for the first time in my life, I was tempted to use weed and alcohol to calm my mind. No one wanted to sell me weed or buy it for me because they saw me as a man of God. I eventually figured out a way to get it, and one night, after smoking it, I woke up feeling paranoid and uncertain. I kept wondering if that was the day I would not make it back home. I kept asking the mother of my children if she had any love for me, but I never got an answer. I then understood the quote: **"If a man chooses love over his destiny, he will lose both."**

I reached out to some men of God and told them to join me on a three-day fast for her, and that the hand of the Lord would play this thing out. I told the Lord I was ready to step into my destiny, though I was unsure how it would pan out. She refused to communicate with any of the people of God in my circle because she knew the Lord might show them what she had been up to, even though they already knew. I was the only one who didn't know what was going on, maybe because I never imagined her capable of doing certain things.

CHAPTER 19

The Hard Choices

"The hardest choices require the strongest will."
—Thanos

A few years back, the Lord showed me a dream. A friend of hers was planning to take her to a hotel and drug her for her male friends to do whatever they wanted. I asked her about her birthday plans that morning, and she said a friend was taking her to a hotel. I explained the dream and told her not to go. I was seen as the enemy that morning for sharing that. I would constantly warn her of the dangers lurking in the shadows, but the more I did that, the more I was seen as the enemy. This time around, I decided to hold my peace. I knew it would be hard for me to be silent and let this play out, even though I did not fully understand what was happening.

I decided to allow God to play his hand, and I knew no matter what happened, all things would work out for my good. The Blueprint says so. The disrespect intensified, and I decided to play it cool. She started to stay out late, so I would pick up the boys, take them home, put them to bed, and pray for strength as the situation was clear. She was having the time of her life, and I was sticking to the blueprint of doing good to the one hurting me. I never felt like doing anything, let alone good, but I still gave what I had. Every chance I got, I had breakdowns occasionally, but the Lord kept me strong and saw me through it until He said it was time. I could not point fingers with prophetic dreams being my only evidence, so I held my peace.

One day, while at home, the Lord told me to wash her feet. I got a bucket of water, got the foot scrub and other tools needed, and washed her feet. I took a towel and dried them. I was unsure why the Lord had me do that at the time. This scripture will give you an idea of what is to come.

It was just before the Passover Festival. Jesus knew that the hour had come for him to leave this world and go to the Father. Having loved his own who were in the world, he loved them to the end. The evening meal was in progress, and the devil had already prompted Judas, the son of Simon Iscariot, to betray Jesus. Jesus knew that the Father had put all things under his power, and that he had come from God and was returning to God; so he got up from the meal, took off his outer clothing, and wrapped a towel around his waist. After that, he poured water into a basin and began to wash his disciples' feet, drying them with the towel that was wrapped around him. He came to Simon Peter, who said to him, "Lord, are you going to wash my feet?" Jesus replied, "You do not realize now what I am doing, but later you will understand." "No," said Peter, "you shall never wash my feet." Jesus answered, "Unless I wash you, you have no part with me." "Then, Lord," Simon Peter replied, "not just my feet but my hands and my head as well!" Jesus answered, "Those who have had a bath need only to wash their feet; their whole body is clean. And you are clean, though not every one of you." For he knew who was going to betray him, and that was why he said not every one was clean. (John 13:1-11 - NIV).

Washing her feet was not an easy thing to do, but it was necessary.

CHAPTER 20

The Betrayal

In prayer, I saw a spirit entering my wife. Then I saw this scripture in Luke 22:

Now the Festival of Unleavened Bread, called the Passover, was approaching, and the chief priests and the teachers of the law were looking for some way to get rid of Jesus, for they were afraid of the people. Then Satan entered Judas, called Iscariot, one of the Twelve. And Judas went to the chief priests and the officers of the temple guard and discussed with them how he might betray Jesus. They were delighted and agreed to give him money. He consented, and watched for an opportunity to hand Jesus over to them when no crowd was present. (Luke 22:1-6 - NKJV).

I knew whatever was in the dark would come to light, and I wept bitterly in prayer as my heart felt like it could stop at any moment. I was now suspicious that she had given a warlock access to me. He was planning to take my life by using her to get to me. I just needed proof.

GETTING THE EVIDENCE

Seeing myself standing in a divorce court telling the judge I had visions of an affair would not help me in the dramatic turn of events. I contacted a man of God and told him I was already aware of what was happening. I believe my circle was afraid to tell me everything because they didn't want to hurt my feelings. I told the man of God I already knew what was up, but I wanted confirmation that what I was seeing was accurate. The man of God said to me, *"Your wife is indeed having an affair. She is still with you only because if she leaves now, she cannot support herself financially. The man she is having an affair with does not give her a lot of money."*

I replied, *"Thank you for telling me."* The phone line went silent for a moment.

Then the man of God said, *"The Lord will keep the promises He has made concerning you. You will travel. You will live a blessed and prosperous life, and she will realize she made the biggest mistake of her life."*

After that, I calmly went home, asked her for a call on her phone, connected to her WhatsApp via barcode, downloaded her conversations, and took screenshots of the discussion about the affair. It was then that I saw a message that sent a cold chill down my spine.

CHAPTER 21

Darkness Exposed

I saw a conversation between her and a man of God we both knew. She was telling him that she was with a man who was perfect for her, but he was a wizard. She wanted to know how to get him out of that lifestyle. The man of God advised her to stop the madness and at least wait until she had divorced her husband. With laughing emojis, she said okay.

Time froze, and the weight of the betrayal started to set in. I was home alone, placed my prayer shawl on my head, and began to pray. Then I saw in a vision a heart on an altar, then a dark hand came up with a knife and stabbed the heart. I fell on my face in distress as my prayer shawl was dripping wet. Still, I decided to maintain a level of focus. Pretending I didn't know anything, I got out of the house with enough evidence to get a divorce in my favor.

The Lord revealed the assignment of the warlock to me. His intention was not just to kill me but the entire family. His goal was to remove me, the head and protector of the family, then easily feast on kids. Thinking of my sons in danger, rage consumed me, and I was having difficulty playing cool.

The next day, in a dream, the Lord showed me police officers coming for me if I allowed my emotions to run wild. So, in the morning, I woke up, kept a leveled head, and left some money on the bed as usual. She took it and left, forgot something, turned back, and started to get a bit loud about how long I took to let her back into the house. That was the straw that broke the camel's back. I grabbed her by the neck and rested my knife on her throat. My sons were looking at me. I did not want them to believe this was a normal thing to do as I desired a prosperous future for them. I looked her in the eyes and told her my destiny was too great for me to waste it with her. Then I walked away.

DELILAH

I went to work that morning a broken man. I was constantly breaking down in the bathroom. I could not continue to work, so I went to the manager to tell her the basic information about what was happening. She immediately told me to go home.

I went into the dressing room to change out of my working clothes, and after I put on the watch I got married in, I heard very firmly in my spirit, *"Time is up."* The hand of the Lord was about to move. I started to weep bitterly, not knowing what exactly this meant, but I knew for sure her life was in danger.

When I got home, I saw her coming with police officers who instructed me to get into the car. I did just that, and they took me to the station. I held my peace as they asked me many questions. My reply to the questions asked was, *"Why do you ask me all these questions? Ask the one who filed the report. Ask her what it is that I have done."* I sat there as the officer looked at me.

They turned to her and said, *"It is obvious that this man must have been pushed and provoked to react in the way you said he did. His eyes are full of love."* She kept quiet, too embarrassed to say what the cause was. The officers told us to wait outside as they would soon take us back home. As I sat there in silence, confused at all that was happening, wondering how I could be repaid like this for my years of sacrifice, I got up from that place and decided to walk home. On my way home, I decided to do my best to think clearly for the sake of my sons.

When I got home, God revealed, through one of his servants, that earlier that day, she had a conversion with the warlock, and he told her to have me arrested and charged. He even told her he could kill me if she was willing to work alongside him on this plan. Suddenly, everything made sense to me. He was casting a stony heart/heartbreak spell. This spell causes its victim to suffer to the point where their heart gives out because the pain is amplified by witchcraft.

Now that everything was coming to light, and because the warlock knew that I knew of him, the Lord revealed that he was trying to complete his assignment quickly.

In a vision, I saw him taking my children's mother to a bar and drugging her. He then took her back to his place and sacrificed her on his satanic altar. I wept bitterly before the Lord and begged him to show mercy when I saw this. Despite all the evil that had been done to me, it was not my plan to be able to say, *"I told you so."*

When she got home, I told her everything the Lord had shown me and that she would be a dead woman if she did not stop and repent. She started to confess that the man was a warlock but thought he would change. She even admitted that he said his reason for being in the occult was to protect himself. He had killed a lot of people, and because he killed so many people, he needed protection. He told her that his ring required blood, but she didn't think much of it. She thought he loved her, and he was talking about getting her pregnant. That was when I remembered a dream I had about a year before this ordeal where she had gotten pregnant for someone else. It was such a shocker that in the dream it caused me to collapse and die.

He had planned to get her pregnant and then use witchcraft to cause her to die in childbirth. His plan was obvious, but GOD. When evil conspired against me in the darkness, they forgot one crucial thing: the Lord's Spirit heard their plans.

The betrayal for me was tough. I had invested in this person, traveled with this person, opened up, laughed with, and fed this person, and I never imagined for a moment that this person had another agenda.

CHAPTER 22

Unmasking Satan

The warlock's mask fell off, and he was exposed. He was a worker of darkness who went around wearing a mask. It was revealed that this man had done much evil.

A few years prior, he dated another married woman whose husband committed suicide when he discovered the affair. Then he dropped the woman, who later became mentally unstable after realizing what had happened. This man became a pro at destroying homes, stealing destinies, and covering stars. Sadly, a few Christians will read this book and still doubt the forces of darkness moving through the land. So many choose to be stuck in the religious box while the snake swallows their families whole. The warlock's time is short, but I hope he sees this book before he dies. You can drink all the blood in the land, fly to Haiti every week for more power, drink blood from skulls, and do rituals day and night, but none of that can protect you from the wrath of God that is coming your way. The Lord allowed you to have beef with me so He could deal with you accordingly. Not only has the Lord shown me your death, but He has shown it in multiple dreams to the woman who was once in your web.

There is no way someone coming to lead you in sin can be sent from God. Be not deceived if you are currently involved in this activity.

It may be masked in fun, and you may be having a good time, but you run the risk of your children being destroyed. Not everyone sleeping around is a part of the occult, but you never know who is, and their targets are people of God who are marked for great works. When the enemy could not shake me with the hardship and distress of warfare, they took a different approach and surprised me from an emotional standpoint—attacking what I loved and valued.

I almost gave up after all this surfaced. After failing to protect my family and not expecting things to turn out messy, I convinced myself that I was unworthy to call myself a man of God.

CHAPTER 23

Bitterness

After deciding to leave, I saw that going away too soon would be harmful to my boys. In just a few days, the water was disconnected, and there was no food in the house. If I followed my emotions, it would not benefit my children at all. I got the water reconnected and remained committed to my duties.

Their mother decided to go for deliverance, and many prayers went up for her, with spirits being cast out, etc. But as the days went by, I started to get bitter. I could not lift my head to heaven to pray for even two minutes because I was so upset. All kinds of thoughts began to enter my mind. *"If God knew she had someone else, why did He make me continue to give? Why keep me here? Why make me look like such a fool."* Pride started to surface. A man of God told me to be humble and trust that God would reward me for my obedience, but every day, just seeing her face made me angry. My prayer life dropped, and in my heart, I blamed God for what had happened. My mind was cloudy.

THE ENEMY ATTACKS WHEN YOU ARE BROKEN

In this time of brokenness, I was just going with the waves, and temptations started to come upon me. I would be angry and start swearing in the slightest distress. All I could think about was what had taken place in the past few months. One night, I was lying in bed, and I started to think about all the women who flirted with me and I turned them down. Feeling stupid, I began to agree with the ungodly thoughts. After weeks of no prayer, I was now weak.

I picked up my phone, made a call, and invited someone to chill. We met up, and that was when I made one of the most foolish decisions of my life. After this sexual encounter, when I got to my gate, I immediately started to feel dark spirits entering me, and a wrestling started to take place inside of me. Realizing I was manipulated by emotions of grief, I began to weep, realizing what I had done.

When I walked through the door, I realized I could no longer look down on my children's mother because I had also sinned and fallen short. I went back outside and asked God to deliver me, and it felt as if the Lord took me up and started to shake the foul spirits out as I was being tossed side to side and vomiting nonstop. Although I regretted this encounter, it did humble me and showed me that no matter how good you think you are, you can fall.

Never pause your prayer life because it keeps your mind and thoughts on the things of God. Everything that is happening around you is trying to stop you from praying, and things get complicated if you do because it is your lifeline. Even in this mess, I learned never to give in to despair because once you do, you give yourself over to your lowest instinct and you will make horrible choices.

"Never allow the actions of someone else to cause you to lose your peace."

—*Author Unknown*

CHAPTER 24

The Turning Point

I was at work one day when a woman of God called me to share a troubling dream she had that I had died. She said I should pray for myself and my youngest son as the enemy wanted to take us out.

While at home a few nights after that, I felt this urge to pray, but I brushed it off because I was still battling condemnation. I felt a presence enter the room, and one of my sons started to have a seizure. I grabbed him and I saw his eyes roll back in his head. I cried to God, begging Him to spare the child for I will certainly return to my post if his life is spared. While he was rushed to the hospital, I stayed and prayed, and the Lord rescued him. That was when I realized I did not have the luxury some men have of living an average everyday life.

I have engaged the supernatural too much to live a life of ignorance. Witches and warlocks know who I am. I have done too much damage to their kingdom to fall back. Them coming after my child, who is innocent in all this, was a turning point for me. I would follow the Blueprint. The light at my feet will lead me through the darkness. If the enemy wanted to destroy me so badly, it must be something in my life that has made them so nervous. I became determined to find out what that was.

CHAPTER 25

They Are After Your Children

There is no *"happy ending"* when a marriage ends in divorce and children are involved. Their destiny is either shifted or destroyed. Their grades begin to fall; they start hanging out with the wrong people; there is low self-esteem, no identity, etc. Divorce can be brutal for children when their parents use them as pawns.

Putting pride and ego before a child's well-being happens far too often. Over 70% of convicts were raised in single-parent households. This system is designed to increase the percentage. The snake hates marriages because unity in a home makes it harder for him to access the next generation. The children are the future. People wonder why this generation is hard to deal with. Well, check their upbringing, and you will see why that is. With divorces rising and the escalating gender war on who is to be blamed, the snake is picking up kids like it is at the grocery store. Weak children become weak, and frail adults are driven by emotions. A country driven by emotions is a weak nation that breeds lawlessness.

They did a study with a group of pedophiles, asking them about the types of children they go after. All of them said they went for children who did not have a father around, which is the snake's strategy in this world. Scripture shows that when Moses came into the world, the king ordered that all male babies be killed. When baby Jesus came into this world, the king wanted Him dead. Your precious babies are no different, and the enemy wants them dead because they carry something that is a threat to him.

CHAPTER 26

Becoming the Man God Has Called Me To Be

Many changes have been made in my life after that season. I look nothing like what I have gone through. I decided to add value to my life every day by studying the Blueprint and other books on self-development, learning how to lead and what is required of me to be a great leader. I sought understanding on what makes a man's character respected and admired by all who come in contact with him. I sought mentorship and submitted to spiritual parents so I could learn to be the father my boys need, and learn to be the man my future wife could be proud of. I added value to myself and everyone I encountered, saving marriages worldwide, and encouraging others to believe in marriage again. The biblical marriage is not the one society has dictated.

GROW THROUGH YOUR PAIN

"People change when they are hurt enough to change."
— *Author Unknown*

The question is, will you change for better or worse? Will you grow from your heartache or sink into despair? Will the pain birth purpose in you, or will it prove the naysayers right?

It is okay to weep, and it is okay to be broken, but don't let that become your identity because it will cause people to distance themselves from you. I understand being hurt, but that cannot be your focus all day. For my own peace, I will step back a little. I heard a funny story once about a dog laying on a nail. The dog was obviously in pain because it was groaning, so someone passing by asked the owner, *"What's the matter with your dog?"*

The owner answered, *"He is laying on a nail, and it hurts."*

The passerby replied, *"So why doesn't he get up?"*

The owner answered, *"Well, I guess it doesn't hurt bad enough."*

It hurts enough to complain, but it doesn't hurt bad enough for him to get up and move. Some of us experience the same pain repeatedly because we refuse to grow up. We end up dealing with the same drama, trauma, and toxic environments.

FOOL ME ONCE, SHAME ON YOU. FOOL ME TWICE, SHAME ON ME

"Insanity is doing the same thing over and over, expecting a different result."

—Albert Einstein

There are so many stories of men and women getting married 4-5 times with the same results. You can't put all the blame on the other person, convincing yourself that meeting someone else will make your life better.

Others are taking advantage of your weaknesses because you are unwilling to change. You get played by the same type of men/women repeatedly. The sooner you live the life the Blueprint designed for you to live, the sooner your life will begin to improve, and the right people will start to enter your life.

Adding value to my life every day has been a game-changer for me. I never thought I would write books, mentor individuals, and minister to God's people globally, but I am doing just that. My assignment is to help men become the best version of themselves so they can be better husbands, fathers, and friends to make society a better place for everyone.

I encourage every woman who reads this book to encourage every male in their life to seek mentorship. I only see 3-5 men at 90% of the seminars I attend. While it is fantastic that women are growing in critical areas of life, if the men don't do the same, the women will not have a fair chance in the dating market because the average man is unhealthy, in debt, has terrible hygiene, and, overall, not attractive. Most men are invisible to women who pass them on the streets daily. The truth is, if a man does not love himself, he will not attempt to fix these key areas of his life. This is why, in mentorship, my goal is to help men get into a state of mind to love themselves because only then can they truly love their wives correctly. As a man, you will not get credit for doing anything unless you do it correctly.

In this same way, husbands ought to love their wives as their own bodies. He who loves his wife loves himself. (Ephesians 5:28 – NIV).

BE THE CAPTAIN OF YOUR SHIP

Regardless of what happens on a ship, the captain is held responsible. If the ship hits something or, for whatever reason, it starts to sink, he cannot get off that ship until everyone else gets off. Don't try to figure things out when the ship is already moving at full speed or it is only a matter of time before it is shipwrecked.

I once read a book that said whatever we study for five years or more, we become experts in that area, elevating us above the average person. With that said, studying marriage will put you above the average person. For example, over 60% of marriages end because of money problems, which means getting your finances in order before looking to take such a step or at least having a few goals in obtaining wealth will be beneficial. Over 50% of marriages struggle because of communication issues, so learn how to express yourself maturely in a conversation. Don't let social media or drama movies be your source on how marriages should function. Don't let these people lie and get in your ear, telling you marriages are unnecessary in this generation because that is precisely what the snake wants you to think.

Marriage is a sacred thing that, if done right, can change a nation for the better. The dysfunction we see today is caused by men leaving their homes and women believing they don't need a man in the home, so their daughters grow up not sure how to deal with men, and their sons grow up not sure how to be a man.

CHAPTER 27

My Advice to Women

The snake hates women, and if you look at what is happening around the world, you can see clearly that there is an attack on women. People can't even tell you what makes a woman a woman these days. A woman's identity is mocked and reduced to nothing in some countries. One of God's most precious gifts to man is being reduced to booty calls by society. Like the snake did to Eve, he is tricking women into believing a lie and responding with emotions. If he can manipulate you, he can destroy your home, kids, and future.

Most of my clients in the mentorship program are women, and I have helped many of them make better life decisions. For some reason, some women have never been held accountable by anyone. A woman can be making the biggest mistake of her life that will damage her reputation, home, and children's future, and all she will hear is, *"Yes, do what you want."* This advice typically comes from her peers, but they don't mean her any good. They are even jealous. Like in the garden, the snake is after the woman because he knows how precious a woman is.

A woman who fears the Lord is far more precious than gold, and the enemy knows this, so he brings confusion to the women by adding or subtracting from the Blueprint to get an emotional reaction from the women. If he can get women to make decisions based solely on emotions, he can destroy not just her but her entire household.

It was a woman who requested the head of the prophet, John the Baptist, and it was given to her. He was a prophet who was known throughout the entire land; his head was given to a woman who was barely known in the castle. The snake knows the power of a woman, and this is why he has used many women to bring down great men.

An entire army could not bring down Samson, but Deliah did it so easily. How many men do you know who have achieved or were on the verge of achieving when an adultery scandal brought shame and disgrace upon them? They get caught up in prostitute scandals, human trafficking scandals, and so on.

The snake desires to use the power women carry for his own selfish desires to bring down the men, just like he did in the garden. When Eve ate the fruit, nothing happened. When she brought it to Adam, and he ate it, that was when their sorrows began.

The snake encourages the woman to go against God, and the woman urges the man to go against God, and the snake laughs. When the Architect of this universe was ready to send His Son to this world, the Spirit of the Lord hovered over this earth looking for a woman to bring fruit to His plan in this world. Do you see how valuable you are as a woman? I have seen men decide to end their own lives because they decided that life without a woman is not worth living. A woman can build or destroy her house, and it is clear that women can shape their home into paradise or hell on earth.

The wise woman builds her house, but with her own hands the foolish one tears hers down. (Proverbs 14:1 – NIV).

This world we live in will not only applaud a woman for tearing down her house but reward her for doing so by putting the tools in her hands. After having an affair, a woman can decide if the father sees the kids, keeps the house, etc. This happens to some men at a point in life where starting over is not even possible, and they end up dead or useless.

Not only can a woman destroy her home, but she has the power to be the one who builds it. The entire household reflects a woman's mood. If you are angry, sad or happy, it reverberates through the entire house, and that is the kind of power you have. Choose to build your house up. Choose to be the woman God called you to be and resist what society wants you to be.

The snake is coming for the very identity of the woman. Value marriage and value purity. Do not allow men with no intentions of staying around to enter your body and throw you to the curve like used napkins. Use biblical standards to decide if a man is for you. Just because a man feeds you, checks up on you, and entertains you, does not mean he sees his end with you.

I raise chickens, and every morning, I check on them, feed them, and make sure they are as comfortable as can be, but rest assured, I am only using these chickens to benefit my personal needs. It does not end well for them. Don't let anyone treat you like a chicken. The perfect man doesn't exist, and just because a man treats his woman right, that doesn't mean he will treat you the exact same way. Don't go looking for the perfect relationship, but equip yourself to be able to build the relationship that is perfect for you.

If your spouse currently has 80% of what you desire, then going out there seeking the other 20% will eventually turn around and leave you with zero. Often, the man who has the 20% you go looking for isn't even half the man who has the 80% you already have.

I remember hearing about a lady in a community who left her husband to run off with a man she thought was her knight in shining armor. When she found out she had cancer and started to lose weight to the point she could no longer walk, her knight in shining armor packed her up, took her back to her husband, and left her there. The husband was the one taking her to the doctor, bathing her, and caring for her until she died. It is not just a cliché: not all that glitters is gold, and watering the grass on your side is much more rewarding than being concerned about the grass on the other side.

ABUSE

No form of abuse is normal, and it should never be seen as such. Too many people use marriage as an excuse to stay in an abusive relationship, and that is definitely not what God wants for you.

YOUR MOUTH

Your words can build your spouse or destroy him. You might not fight him physically, but your words can have the same effects as him putting his hands on you. If you can master speaking to your spouse to get him to respond the way you want, it is a life changer. Your mouth has the power to cause him not to want to come home or to want to rush home.

> **Better to live on a corner of the roof than share a house with a quarrelsome wife. (Proverbs 21:9 – NIV).**

This is not saying you should speak to your husband like a child because he is not. You should talk to your husband with respect. Why is it so easy to talk to your boss, pastor, etc. respectfully, but the man willing to die for you is seen as less than any of these men? Your boss would not give blood to save you. Your boss would not give you his last meal. Your boss would not give his life for you. If you die today, your boss will seek someone else to take your place. You may be working for a boss who is disrespectful to you, but every day, you go to work ready to obey that boss, yet you disrespect your man at home. Why is that? Do you think God is pleased? Would you be comfortable seeing a woman treat your son the way you treat your husband? What words of advice would you give your brother or a close male relative being treated the way you treat your husband?

YOUR MINDSET

Many of the challenges you face in your marriage are a result of your mindset. Entering a marriage with the *"I'm a strong, independent woman who doesn't need a man mindset"* will not end well. If I applied for a job and, in the interview, my words were, *"I'm a strong, independent person who doesn't need a job,"* the employer would not hire me because, obviously, he would have a hard time working with such a person. Can you blame him for not wanting to work with such a person?

As a businesswoman, would you partner with someone who constantly tells you they don't need your partnership? Even if you are responsible for their five-dollar increase in sales, you still want to feel like you add some form of value to the partnership. If a man asks you to marry him, he is asking you to partner with him, and you can accept or decline the partnership. Would it make sense to accept the terms and conditions of the partnership and then hop out when emotions run high? If your mindset towards marriage is that it is just a piece of paper, then marriage is not for you. If all you think about is the big wedding and your ex being jealous because social media is flooded with you in a pretty dress to prove the haters wrong, I am sure divorce is coming. Would you open a business just to take pictures of it without actually planning to commit to that business? Are you seeking stability or praise? Ask yourself the tough questions about marriage; if you are not sure you want to marry, don't. Not everyone is destined for marriage, and that is okay.

To those rushing their daughters into marriage, please stop pressuring them to get married because getting married *"late"* is better than being married to the wrong person. It is better to have your daughter there with you than for her to feel pressured into a marriage that might return her to you in a body bag.

A woman's body might get a man to look her way, but once he sees the way she thinks, he has already decided if it is worth it or not. Too many women have this mindset that once they become successful, that makes them attractive. What you find attractive in a man is not the same qualities men seek in a spouse. Only weak men seeking an opportunity to use you will come your way, and they will take your car and will always ask you for money because they are playing the feminine role, leaving you wondering where are the real men because, eventually, you get tired of giving. At the start of that relationship, you will treat that man exactly how you want to be treated (subconsciously). Then you become frustrated when you realize he has no plans on reciprocating.

Become a successful woman because you want to, not because you think it will make you more attractive to a man you desire. This world is full of successful single women, but it is not their success that makes them single but the attitude that comes with the success that some women allow to make them act a certain way. Please investigate what is required to be with the man you desire. Is he looking for a woman like you? Keep in mind that a man is not looking for the same attributes you find attractive in a man.

THE IDOLS OF YOUR HEART

Women, be careful of the idols you allow your heart to worship because having an idol is a sin. Some women's idols are men over 6 feet. They don't care how good a man is. If he is not over 6 feet, they are not interested. Some women idolize men with big ding dongs.

There she lusted after her lovers, whose genitals were like those of donkeys and whose emission was like that of horses. (Ezekiel 23:20 – NIV).

When you refuse to give up your idols, God will give you over to your idols because they have become your god. This is how you think you found the perfect man, and then time reveals your knight in shining armor is a devil in disguise who has done nothing but bring pain and suffering to your life. You worship these idols in your heart.

For some, a dildo has become an idol. It is all you think about, and it is the first thing you reach for when your eyes open in the morning before you even check if you can get up out of bed and walk. Now you find it hard to receive pleasure from your spouse because your idol, the dildo, has taken his place. It is okay to have desires, but don't let your preference become an idol in your heart. You stand a better chance of getting your desired spouse when your preferences are not your idol. The only perfect man you will find is Jesus Christ. Far too many people are profiting from lying to and preying on women's emotions. They tell you what will make you applaud them, buy their books, and tune in to their podcasts. The truth is like bitter herbs, but it will heal you from the inside and out.

Choose a man based on his character and not only what he has. If you desire a man with a house, car, nice clothes, etc., you can be tricked because some men will have these things and have ill intentions towards you. Does he believe in biblical principles? Is he trustworthy? Does he love and respect his parents? Is he a man of his word? Is he ambitious? Does he have a vision for his life? These things matter more than material stuff; if he possesses good qualities, then the material things will come.

I told my children's mother that I couldn't stop her from going out there seeking a man, but I told her that her mindset was not right, and that is why she got played. Her morals were wrong, and it almost cost us our lives. I was as straightforward as I could be. Some men out there are ready to use any woman they can, so I told her, for the sake of the children, to make better choices. Desire a man who will treat you and your children right instead of using you and treating them ill. I was told I was too judgmental for saying these things, but like some women, she just doesn't want to be held accountable because that would require change. It is easier for a woman to say men are trash instead of admitting they have been dating or are interested in the wrong type of men. You can be seriously hurt if you choose a man based on emotions and what you see.

COMPETITION

I have no idea why women compete with each other so much. Do you think it is wise to take advice from someone who might be secretly competing with you? This could be anyone, even your mother. I have seen mothers who are jealous of their daughter's marriage plant evil seeds in the union. Some women do this subconsciously without even being aware of it.

If you are married, it is wise to move around with other married women because your single friends will give single advice in the hope you act single and ultimately join them. I have seen women who have been friends for years try and crawl into their best friend's bed to get their husbands. They may invite you to places no married woman should go and may even try to set you up on a guy, hoping you sleep with this guy or fall in some way to feel better about herself for not having the things you have. There are women in their forties trying to get the same men as the women in their twenties. This competition is so bitter.

Some women will belittle other women. Even though my children's mother considered the marriage a waste of time years ago, a few of her friends were so jealous. They felt she was too young to be married and have a family, etc. Keep your eyes and ears open, and you will see the secret competitors in your life.

Remember, misery loves company, so be careful of the advice you follow. Some of the women I see encouraging women to live life without a man are actually married. They say these things knowing it is what women love to hear, and they can profit from it.

"Be a strong, independent woman who doesn't need a man to keep chasing the bag."

They sell this advice, then go home to their husbands. These women are role models for a lot of young women. Don't stand too close to women whom the man you desire finds repulsive. You could be an innocent woman, but if you keep company with women who are promiscuous, you might be labeled as one.

YOU DO NOT NEED A MAN TO BE A WIFE

There are some women who are married but are not yet wives.

He who finds a wife finds a good thing, and obtains favor from the Lord. (Proverbs 18:22 – NKJV).

Before that man asks you to marry him, you should already be a wife. You already know what it means to be a wife. After marriage, he should not have to tell you that your clothing is too revealing because you were already covered up when he found you. You already possess the qualities the Blueprint says you should have as a wife.

Like a gold ring in a pig's snout is a beautiful woman who shows no discretion. (Proverbs 11:22 – NIV).

Beauty fades in marriage. Eventually, it won't be enough, but your character, cooking, and the peace you give your husband will keep him bragging. All some men have to show for their investment is a woman with a big butt, which is not what a wife is.

If you are married and you find yourself struggling for a long period of time, then something is not right. I was broke for most of my marriage. My finances were so bad that I was sleeping on cardboard while the children and their mother were on the bed. I tried taking out loans; I tried saving; I tried everything that came to mind to get a bed to no avail. Immediately after the affair and the covenant was broken, I got a bed, fan, dresser, and big-screen TV. My life has been an uphill journey since then. If you saw how I dressed then compared to how I dress now, you would see a big difference. The Lord always wanted to bless me, but He won't bless confusion and disorder.

If you are a married woman and not a wife to your husband, you are delaying the fruits of both your labor. Often, my clients express to me that they won't submit or be wives to their husbands because they are not earning what their friends' spouses earn, etc. That is not a valid excuse to look down on your husband, and with that mindset, he will not climb any higher. Never hit a man when he is down because he will never forget it.

A lady once shared a story about how she watched her husband pray for the womb of barren women to be open, and all the women got pregnant. At the same time, she sat at home childless. One day, she said enough is enough. When her husband came home, she washed his feet, sat before him, and repented for dishonoring him. She submitted herself before him and asked him to pray for her, and that is when her story changed. She decided to be a wife; the house was now in order and positioned for the blessing.

Be a wife before you are found so that when you are found, you won't need to figure out how to be a wife. You may be reading this chapter with a bad taste in your mouth, but please don't skip over this because your feelings are hurt. You would never ignore a life-saving surgery because it hurts, so don't ignore this chapter. Think hard about the man you choose to give yourself to. You are too valuable to give yourself to a man who doesn't see himself being with you for the rest of his life. Being a good woman won't cure a man's mental illness or past traumas. That is something he must address for himself. You can be a good woman with or without a man.

UNFORGIVENESS AND BITTERNESS

Unforgiveness and bitterness are responsible for some women living miserable lives. Your spouse hurt you, and you can't ignore that he did, but if he genuinely apologized for it and is doing better, why hold him hostage? If he has changed, why hold the same old image of him before you and hold on to the grudge? One of the most significant issues that caused my ordeal was that my wife still saw me as the same man who hurt her years prior. I was growing right before her eyes, and she couldn't see it because she was holding on to bitterness.

Simple discussions would blow up into something big. If keeping grudges and keeping score is something you do, then marriage might not be for you. No man constantly wants to be reminded of his past mistakes, especially a man doing his best to become a better version of himself. Don't let unforgiveness rob you of a good life.

Every so often, women ask, *"What do men want?"* but as soon as they start to hear what is being said, they disagree and start saying things like *"but..." "if..."* and *"I just feel..."* Then, when a man is not interested or loses interest in a short time, they wonder why.

I had the privilege of having businesswomen in the mentorship program, and this really opened my eyes to the fact that boss chicks desire love like every other woman out there. Some of these women were actually married but carried the burden of running a business alone and just wanted the husband to take the lead so they could kick their feet up, relax, and be taken care of.

CHAPTER 28

My Advice For Men

Every projection of hell is against men. The snake did not come to Adam in the garden, but he went for the weaker vessel. In today's world, the enemy is still doing that. The suicide rate among males in 2021 was approximately four times higher than the rate among females. Males make up 50% of the population but nearly 80% of suicides.

The great Roman Empire fell because men became inflamed with lust. We see men today caught up in this very trap. Some men's only goal is to figure out when to *"bust"* the next nut. Sex is all some men think about because they are programmed to think like this—sex sells. You can't even see a commercial about glasses without a woman showing her body parts. You see an ad pop up, and it is about sex. You see a flyer on a wall advertising a cookout, but for some reason, naked women are on the flyer, distracting the men from their purpose with sexual images. There are not enough people talking about sexual addiction, and too many are struggling and ashamed to seek help.

THE PORN INDUSTRY AND ADDICTION

Pornography is a multi-billion dollar industry that benefits from the destruction of the younger generation. One of the purposes of porn is to open the door to cause you to start thinking like a gay. If you watch five porn scenes, that is five male genitalia you have seen, and your brain is like a hard drive that stores information. After a year of porn, how many male genitalia would be embedded on your hard drive? The snake can't kill all the men in the world, so he makes the ones he can't kill weak by messing up their mental hard drive. So many women are married to men who are addicted to porn, and that is a key ingredient for an affair that will contribute to a divorce. If you are struggling in this area, you must break this addiction. Only then will you be free to be the man you are destined to be.

Sexual immorality is one of the biggest issues holding men back from becoming the best version of themselves. Samson could defeat an entire army with a donkey's jawbone, but it took one woman to defeat him. When you see great men like Samson fall, you must gird up your loins, for you are no greater than him. If he could be tempted, so can you. So many find it easier to satisfy themselves instead of working on themselves so they can find a wife to satisfy them.

IDOLS OF YOUR HEART

With the help of pornography, butts and breasts have become the idol for many men. They bend a knee and physically worship some of these women. Imagine choosing a woman to spend the rest of your life with, and you make that decision based on the size of her butt and breast. Does she add value to your life? How is her mentality and morals? Looking at a woman and saying she is wife material because of her looks alone costs many men their sanity. Fall in love with her roots because her flowers will fade away in the winter.

Do not lust in your heart after her beauty or let her captivate you with her eyes. (Proverbs 6:25 – NIV).

Don't let a woman's beauty or physique become your heart's idol because that will blind you to your decisions.

For some men, their job/money is their idol. They neglect their family to focus completely on work, which eventually leads to the destruction of the home.

EMOTIONS

You don't want to be an overly emotional man because that is also a state of weakness. If your feelings are stronger than your will, your life will continue to be brutal. I am not saying your emotions are not valid. I am saying they should not control you. I have seen men walk out of their children's lives because their emotions convinced them that their bitterness should keep them away because the mother did them wrong. So many men are behind bars because they could not overpower their emotions. Don't be a slave to your emotions because it will make you a poor leader. You might not feel like following the Blueprint, but you must if you desire to live a fulfilled life.

A young lady messaged me one day after she saw me encouraging other men to get it together. She said, *"My former male friend and father have an issue with males telling them how to be men. Neither one of them likes to take accountability and would rather just have people who cuddle them and tell them that everything will be okay or just 'yes' men who will agree with their behavior. It is hard telling women they are wrong, and it is even harder telling a man who acts like a woman that they are wrong because of womanly tendencies and misplaced male aggression. Please continue trying to help these men because when you help men, you are also protecting women."* There are emotional men who don't want to acknowledge their faults.

THE FUNCTIONS OF A MAN

Men are expected to provide and protect. As a man, you should desire the need to do these things.

PROTECT

You are expected to provide protection physically, mentally, and spiritually.

It is hard to protect your family when you are a nice guy. I have mentored men who would tell me how nice they are, but they are either rejected or used. I sympathize with them because I have been there. Nice guys are normally very passive, with not many boundaries in place. Being saved doesn't mean being soft. Being a believer doesn't mean you say yes to everything and agree with everyone. Jesus Christ stood before thousands of people and told them the truth. He was never afraid to do so, nor should you be afraid. The very woman you love will test your boundaries. No one should feel comfortable disrespecting your family. No boy should feel comfortable speaking to your wife or daughters any way he feels in your presence. You should be a man capable of defending your family if the situation should arise. It doesn't hurt to learn boxing, martial arts, etc.

PROTECT YOUR HEALTH

Protecting your health is also protecting your family mentally. Eating yourself into an early grave is traumatic for your family when they have to watch sickness bring you down to your knees, and you can no longer help yourself. Your wife now becomes the family's breadwinner. I have seen men who lose their health also lose their family and self-respect.

I once saw a man who became an alcoholic after becoming ill and he could no longer walk or talk well after being stuck in bed. He was downstairs while his wife was upstairs with another man. He was a very nice man, but his wife would always rule over him long before he got sick. What a terrible way to go; sick and helpless knowing another man is in your house. I advise you to protect your health so you can be there for your family for a long time. Many men leave their families before time because of sicknesses that can be avoided by investing in their health.

MENTAL HEALTH

Your mental health plays a huge role in how your family functions. If your mind is not in order, your house will not be in order. If you have trauma dealing with, then seek a professional therapist. Receive the mind of Christ.

I saw an interview with a famous pro wrestler, Sting. He was a WWE Hall of Famer. He talked about his battle with depression and that no amount of money or drugs could bring him out of his despair. In the eyes of his fans, he was on top of the world, but he was at his lowest. Your family might see you and think everything is okay, but you are one step away from a complete breakdown. Don't wait until that happens before you seek help.

Men, you are to protect your family from worldly corruption and teach your children right from wrong. If you stand as a man and resist worldly influence, then your family will be safe.

PROVIDE

Just because you were raised seeing your mother as the sole provider of the house does not mean she wanted it to be that way, and that doesn't mean that is how it should be. I have spoken to many women who do a great job securing the bag, but they get tired and would love to be taken care of and not be the one to always figure everything out.

Money is one of the biggest reasons for divorce, which cannot be ignored. Fifty years ago, a man could have a simple job and still be able to take care of his family. It is not that simple today with the cost of living increasing. Most people will judge you based on what you can provide, and women don't usually date downwards.

As a man, you can date an unemployed woman who is not doing well. You can date her because you are not looking for a provider. In most cases, a woman can be unemployed for years, and it wouldn't bother a man who has his finances together, but if a man loses his job, he knows it is only a matter of time before his woman starts to act a certain way. People treat a man differently when he is unable to provide, so getting your finances in order is vital as a man. A good woman will stand by you on bad days, but she is not designed to carry that burden all her life, so be intentional about your money.

EMOTIONAL SUPPORT

Men are expected to provide emotional support as well. Women are very emotional. You don't want her to be expressive with any other man but you. Learn to listen and learn to communicate correctly. It will benefit your children as well. Be a man of your word. Whatever you tell your family you will take care of, make sure you come through on that promise.

SPIRITUAL INSIGHT

Being able to provide spiritual wisdom to your wife is good. Teaching her the things of the spirit is good and beneficial to the household. Some women who are married to pastors cannot quote ten scriptures but are seen as first ladies in their church. Before running to tell the church what God has revealed to you, teach it to your wife and children first. Protect your family from spiritual attacks by providing a solid covering.

SIDE CHICK OR SIDE HUSTLE

Imagine how much further you can go if you invest your time and money in something you can profit from. If you can afford junk food, you can afford a gym membership. It is all about priorities; you must decide what is important and be honest with yourself. If your marriage sucks, finding another woman to keep on the side won't help solve the problem you have at home. It doesn't matter how many nations a king conquers if his home is a battlefield and there is no peace. I will explain more in my next book, ***"Being a Man of Value."*** Helping just one man to become a better person means he becomes a better husband, brother, neighbor, friend, father, son, son-in-law, etc.

TAKE PRIDE IN YOURSELF

Getting married is not a license to stop being concerned with your appearance and body odour. Taking care of your responsibilities should not mean totally abandoning yourself. Often, you think your spouse is not in the mood, but she is just not in the mood for you. I have married women in the mentorship program who are very honest enough to tell me the truth. Since I experienced this firsthand as well, I know what I am saying is true.

A few years after I got married, my nephew, about thirteen years old then, looked at me and said, *"I will never get married."*

"Why?" I asked him.

"Because you started to look awful ever since you married," he replied.

That should have been a wake-up call for me from the start.

LEADERSHIP

As men, we need to study leadership because everything I mentioned above will require us to be good leaders. Before you start demanding change from your spouse, be sure to demand changes from yourself first. Make personal changes before you even start to consider asking others to change.

If your spouse refuses your leadership or sees it unfit for her and does not respect your boundaries, then it is a sign that she might not be the woman for you, and that does not mean she is a bad person; it just means she is not the one for you. If she decides to be with someone else, you must believe that it was not an accident because women think day and night about their next move. She compared you to the other man and found you lacking, then took a bet that she had a much better chance at life with the other man than she has with you. When you are aware of that, there is no need to try and force her to see that you are a better choice for her.

Stop trying to force others to get on your program. Stop talking if she is not listening. If you stop talking to people who are not listening to you and start watching them instead, you will see their motives. You can't make people change by giving them more of what they don't appreciate. Being a good man will not cure your spouse's mental illness or past trauma. They must take care of that by taking the necessary healing protocols.

RESPECT

You can't lead without respect. Even if you don't like your boss, as long as you respect him/her, it doesn't bother them because they know the work will be done, and you are open to suggestions. I learned this from my experience interacting with so many married couples in our mentorship program. It is not that the husband doesn't have good ideas, but the wife often doesn't respect him. I have spoken to women who will say they don't love their husbands but still respect them, and that respect causes them to still function as a wife. Still, another will tell me she loves her husband, but she doesn't respect him, so there is an affair. If there is no affair, the husband is often treated pretty poorly. For example, sex that should be regular for a married man becomes a Christmas gift. He has to consider himself *"lucky tonight."*

While writing, I got a message from a man asking if I have any open slots for the mentorship program. When I asked him if he was okay, he told me his wife of over twenty years was having an affair. My heart skipped a beat because I knew this was another broken man falling victim to the snake's system. Being a good man won't keep you from things like this, but a respected and valued man has less chance of this kind of open disrespect.

WHY BECOME A PERSON OF VALUE?

Most women will consider their options before leaving or cheating. Most of the time, the man she cheats with is better off than the man she is currently with, even if her current partner has a better character. If she chooses vanity over character, she will choose the man doing better. If you use nice things to get her, she will choose someone with nicer things. She will leave if she is not the type to cheat but has already considered that she can find better. Does this make her a bad person? No, it does not. But this is why a number of men are abandoned during a dark time in their lives. Not all women will do this, but I am shedding light on this area because it does happen.

Looking back on my life, the affair happened at my lowest point in life. I was on the floor, and all my money was spent keeping the house running. I was going up against witches near and far. It felt like I was in quicksand, and seeing me at my worst was when she decided she could do better. Being influenced by others helped with that decision.

"A woman's loyalty is tested when a man has nothing; a man's loyalty to his woman is tested when he has everything."

—unknown.

While a woman is still very young and unwise, she will do an evaluation and see that she doesn't have much to lose. This is good and bad news. The bad news was that my wife chose someone else while I was at the lowest point of my life. All my efforts and years of sacrifice were seen as nothing, and she decided that this man was better than the man she was married to. The man was known, older, and financially stable, with a house, car, etc. I was at such a low place in life, but I still hoped that she would have a change of heart.

The good news is that this happened to me before the age of thirty and before the promises of God started to manifest in my life. While she had me on a scale, the Lord also had her on a scale. She found me not fit to be with, and the Lord found her unfit to go where He is taking me. It broke my heart but opened my eyes. I was being compared to someone older than me, understanding that most men, as they get older, slowly start to get their life in order, so the comparison in stature wouldn't be the best to decide who she was better off with. It may have felt like the best decision at the moment but time would have proven otherwise. As the Lord started to open doors for me, I realized that becoming a person of value limits the amount of nonsense you tolerate, and this is why I help men and women become better versions of themselves.

You need to bring so much value to your relationships that people must think twice about losing you. Learn how to think critically, knowing every decision has a consequence. As a man, I urge you to stop seeking happiness. I have observed the lives of men who are successful and unsuccessful. Successful men seek a fulfilled life, while unsuccessful men are stuck in their emotions, battling depression because no one loves them. They feel invisible, so they leach on to bad habits, unhealthy food and people to feel happy, even for a minute.

The greatest man to ever walk this earth, King Jesus, came to this realm with determination and focus to fulfill His purpose, not to feel happy. On the cross, before His last breath, He said, *"It is finished."* Seeking happiness is how some men end up with addictions because they want to feel good. You know the woman doesn't love you; you know she is not an asset to your life, but she makes you feel good, so you hang on to her until, like meth, she causes you to rot from the inside out. When the things that give you temporary happiness leave, you end up wanting to take your life. Death comes so quickly after retirement because, without purpose, the will to live becomes passive.

CHAPTER 29

Take Control of Your Life

Your life is how it is because of your choices. Stop pointing fingers at everyone else and start accepting responsibility for your actions. The sooner you do, the more power you will have to make life-changing decisions.

There is a version of you that is healthy, respected, loved, good with finances, dresses well, etc., but to be that person will require you to give up the person you are right now.

My painful season required me to focus on what I wanted and who I needed to be. When my male clients often complain that their family doesn't respect them, their wives don't want to have sex with them anymore, etc., my response is always *"Sad, but it's good."* All this indicates is that there is room for much more growth, and pain is the fuel to take them to the next level.

When that affair happened, and I realized how I almost lost my life, things started to change rapidly. I would normally complain that I don't have enough time to exercise, but after that pain came into my life, I was out of the house by 4 a.m. running. I started to accept and hold on to that pain and use it to turn my life around. The enemy intended to kill me, but all he did was push me to step into my calling. I took full responsibility for everything that happened and was determined to make the decisions that would make my life better, not bitter. This is the mindset I strive to get my male clients to understand.

The people we admire in this life who have risen to great heights did so because they overcame a level of trauma that could have destroyed them but didn't. My Lord Jesus Christ came to earth and suffered. They gave Him a crown of a thorns, but in the end, He got a crown declaring Him King of kings. We celebrate Him because He overcame everything, and He wants you to do the same.

CHAPTER 30

Marriage

Keep in mind that whatever is in you will be squeezed out once you get married. If adultery is in you, then marriage will bring it to the forefront. If anger is in you, then your marriage will squeeze it out of you, and blaming someone else for what is in you is a delusion.

In the year 2020, when the Lord spoke through His servant, my spiritual father, William Tyrone Jackson, to deliver a word, I was unsure how that would be possible, but as time went by, the word came to pass. The word was, *"The Lord said He's going to use you to help many marriages to function properly."* When this word was spoken, I said, *"Lord, my own marriage is in shambles. How will I be able to help anyone get their marriage right?"* It was much later that the revelation came.

When you are bitten by a snake, the doctors will always ask this question, *"Did you see the snake that bit you?"* If you can identify the snake that bit you, then they know what anti-venom to give. The cure is in the venom. Many people keep falling into bad relationships because they cannot identify the snake that bit them in the first failed relationship. In every other relationship they enter, they still have that toxic venom that pollutes the relationship. I saw the snake that bit me, and the cure was from that snake bite. It didn't kill me, but it made me become a better man. Like the Apostle Paul, he was bitten, and the snake bite caused him great pain, but it didn't kill him. The bite from this snake caused me great pain and sleepless nights, but it didn't kill me.

Now I help others to avoid the same mistakes I made and also the mistakes others have made. When we see marriages failing, we should get out a notebook, take notes, and learn instead of believing, *"That could never be me."* You are not exempt from the same temptations and challenges everyone else faces.

Marriage is a beautiful thing that the Lord designed to bring a man and a woman together. The snake seeks to destroy this sacred thing. We should do our best to expose all the lies and attacks the enemy is throwing at marriages in this generation to try and discourage the idea of ever getting married. He fights marriages between men and women but encourages marriage between the same gender.

If you are married, but your marriage is going through a rough season—if your marriage is bleeding—the clock is ticking, and you must seek wisdom on how to stop the bleeding before it bleeds out. Don't take advice from the world that says follow your heart because your heart will lead you to a place where temporality feels good, but it will bring even more pain and suffering.

Getting married to the right person is more important than getting married before thirty. Marriage can be why you fail at life or excel, which should cause you to pray long and hard about who you spend your life with.

Before you get your driver's license, you are given a road code book, followed by a driving test because they know how serious knowing the road code is to prevent fatal accidents, so they get you as knowledgeable as possible. Study the Blueprint before you even think about getting that vehicle called marriage.

When that check light comes on in your car, you take the necessary precautions to get it fixed, so please do not ignore the check light in your marriage when it comes on. A car doesn't need just gas to function. It needs more to keep it running smoothly, so don't think love is enough to keep your marriage going smoothly for fifty years without regular servicing.

As iron sharpens iron, so one person sharpens another. (Proverbs 27:17 – NIV).

If you are iron, but your partner is wood, then the iron will break the wood into pieces. If both of you are iron, then you will sharpen each other. The sooner you understand this, the better things will get.

Marriage has never stopped a man or woman from having an affair. In the old days, a woman caught in adultery would be stoned to death, but that law didn't stop some of them from doing it anyway. Please understand, nothing you do can make or stop someone from cheating. It comes down to their character and the fear of God in them.

I saw a young lady giving marriage advice to other women on social media. She was saying, in a nutshell, marriage is nothing and that other women should leave their marriages. This woman was a porn star with two failed marriages. Misery loves company indeed. I advise married couples to limit their time on social media and listening to individuals like that young lady. That will add to the confusion in your marriage, and social media is filled with people with that mindset. The wedding day is the start, not the finish line. Keep that in mind, and don't go digging in a coal mine expecting to find gold. It is wise to have someone who keeps you accountable.

Is the person you desire to marry accountable to anyone who can be honest enough to tell you if they think the person is ready for marriage? Respectfully, I took advice from a few men of God who were very passive. There are men who fear God and live honest lives, but they are not strong leaders. Their advice would always be to go with the flow because *"a happy wife means a happy life."* I loved these men. Some of them played a huge role in my walk with the Lord, but when I was told to overlook everything and stay in the marriage, I refused because I remembered what the Lord told me. To them, it was okay because it was a matter they put up with in their own homes. Their wives didn't respect them as men. I had to respectfully end a few relationships in that season and draw closer to men who were leaders, not just in church but in their homes as well.

One of the biggest challenges I see happening in this generation is that too many butterflies are married to worms. There are people who are caterpillars dating worms. A caterpillar is comfortable going around on the ground until, after a while, he/she matures into a butterfly, only to realize the other person (worm) is bound to the ground. Marry someone who is fit for the journey and not just for the season you are in.

DIVORCED

The Blueprint tells us that the Lord hates divorce.

> **"For the Lord God of Israel says that He hates divorce, for it covers one's garment with violence," says the Lord of hosts. "Therefore take heed to your spirit, that you do not deal treacherously." (Malachi 2:16 – NKJV).**

Divorce is an ugly thing that robs innocent children of having a life with mom and dad being there to support them. The children are the real victims of divorce. The Lord does not rejoice to see this happen. People walk into marriage and destroy the children, thinking such wickedness is overlooked because it is not their fault. Every tear from that child will fall on your head, and unless you repent, it will not go well with you. While these children are so vulnerable, they are being introduced to several partners that mom/dad brings around them in a short space of time. Sad to say, this is where many innocent children have suffered abuse—sometimes in secret—for years.

Sometimes I lose sleep at night just thinking about what would have happened if I did not know the Lord and if He hadn't revealed the enemy's plans to me. What if I had found out about the affair and left, then she moved in with that man and took the children there to live? What torture would they endure?

The Bible is clear on the acceptable grounds for divorce.

> **But I tell you that anyone who divorces his wife, except for sexual immorality, makes her the victim of adultery, and anyone who marries a divorced woman commits adultery. (Matthew 5:32 – NIV).**

There is only one exception for divorce. Too many people are getting divorced for reasons not mentioned in the Blueprint. *"I'm no longer happy"* is not a reason for a divorce.

People need to learn how to work on their marriages while being unhappy. No man or woman should believe they have a chance to get with you because you are not happy. I am sure you still work to provide for your family, even when you feel like giving up. If someone asked if you would quit your job and stay home because you were not happy, you would tell that person to get lost because you know happiness is not what you need for an income. Yet so many people have deliberately ended their marriages because they feel sad. Some men look at sad married women like lions look at a wounded zebra—an easy kill. They look at some women like an ox—she is too powerful to take down, and the only way to get a chance is to separate her from the herd because the herd will protect her. Women who are held accountable by other mature women or men are a much harder target to bring down. Hence, some men will go for the sad women. So, before the snake tries to seduce you, it tries to manipulate you because it is trying to get you to be committed to your emotions rather than the facts.

"I'm no longer attracted to my spouse" is not a green light to sleep with someone else. Do you pack up and leave your house when you see a few cracks? No, you repair the damage and get some paint to give it a fresh look. There are men who risk losing their families for a woman they barely know. If your partner cheats and breaks the covenant you made before God, you don't have to stay. You have a legal right to leave. When you sign a business contract, there are terms and conditions that warn you that the contract can be terminated if you step outside the agreement. I see many people sit

in marriage and accept being constantly cheated on. That cannot be good for your mental health.

The Lord does not desire for you to endure constant disrespect. I prayed to the Lord to free me if He saw that my wife would not change, though I was unaware that certain things would have to take place for that to happen. When you pray for the rain, you must also deal with the mud.

David was God's will for Israel, but they got Saul first. If you were married to Saul, and all he/she has been doing is trying to kill you—maybe not physically but spiritually—when they decide to take themselves out of the way, the Lord has your David prepared—someone after His own heart.

"We're just not compatible" is also not a reason to get a divorce. God will help make it work if both agree they want it to. God will not force it to work. One person cannot make it work, but only if the two unite. God honors marriage, so even if you believe you got married to the wrong person, if that person is willing to let God lead, it will be well. If they refuse God, then there is nothing you can do.

Whatever problem is being faced, if Jesus is invited in, He can fix things. If money is the issue, He can fix it. If you are struggling to get pregnant, He can fix it. If you're incompatible, Jesus can fix it.

Listening to Pastor Myles Munroe's teachings on marriage is an eye-opener. He said most marriages face challenges every seven years. After seven years, a married couple will become familiar with each other, and familiarity breeds contempt. Starting to treat your spouse like they are just the average Joe you see every day is a disaster waiting to happen. My marriage lasted seven years, and if you check the statistics, you will see that many marriages that end do so after seven, fourteen, or twenty-one years because they got tired of their partner. Somebody got bored and felt like the other person would always be there, so they go out and seek what they believe was lacking. This is valuable information. Everything that is built will be tested, and being able to recognize the testing will help the marriage stand. So when your marriage is under attack, that attack has come to reveal what is against you and show you who is with you.

Growing in a marriage is essential because if one is blind, they won't see the attack, and hatred for the other will creep in.

I remember a very vivid dream I had in 2020. In this dream, I spoke with a dark entity who told me the attacks would not stop until he destroyed my marriage. I asked, *"Why?"*

He said, *"I will be promoted."*

He had an assignment. He was sent, and he had rank.

Marriage is war, but it is up to you to find out who you are against and know your enemy because your enemy knows you. If you are reading this and thinking it shouldn't or doesn't need all this to make a marriage work, wait until you see and feel the effects of a divorce. Entering a marriage blind is a choice.

"Love won't keep your marriage from falling, knowledge will."
—*Myles Munroe.*

Invest your time and money into materials on marriage. Listen to audiobooks to or from work; buy books on marriage and go to functions that teach about marriage. Through these tools, you will find the importance of date nights, vacations, therapy, and many other important things a marriage needs to be sustained.

Divorce is very painful, and for some men, death seems easier than going through a divorce. I was watching a movie the other day where a soldier got caught behind an enemy line and was being tortured to tell the location of his squad. The interrogator torturing him realized he was not complying, so he said him, *"I see you're no stranger to pain."*

"I've been married twice," replied the soldier. All the men in the room groaned as if to say that even electrocuting him could not be compared to two divorces.

Before I could be of help to people getting a divorce or close to getting it, I really had to address my heart posture before God and ask Him to heal me. I had to get over the affair of my own marriage to be of any help and assistance to even the very people currently in an affair who needed my help. Sitting in a room full of men who were blindsided by a divorce is truly disturbing. Every chance I get to listen, I take notes because these men know something I don't, and after 20-30 years of marriage, I am sure they have a thing or two to say.

SEPARATION

Being separated is not a green light to jump into another relationship with someone else. Many people have been hurt this way. Separation is not a green light to be out there looking for a spouse. This is a time to reflect and heal. There are emotional scars that need to be addressed and dealt with. I have seen people, after a separation, insist on proving to the other person that they made a mistake leaving them, so they go out looking for revenge. They wouldn't go to the gym while married, but now they are at the gym. They wouldn't do their nails and hair while married, but now they are in the salon. One out of four marriages is sexless, but now divorced, sex is all they can think about. It is not bad doing these things, but the motive behind it comes into question. The only person you should take revenge on is your past self—the weaker version of yourself is the one you need to prove wrong.

Many people struggle to find closure while separated. They question the why, how, and what. Unsure of the future, they start looking to the past. The disrespect is all the closure you need to move on sometimes.

Every so often, I would hear someone who is divorced blame the other person for everything that happened. When asked what part they played in their marriage ending, they go quiet. I used the downfall of my marriage as a mirror. I place it before me and examine it from every angle, asking myself the tough questions. What in me made me choose to marry this person? Why did I ignore the signs? Why didn't I address the patterns? Why did I remain in a place I was not respected or celebrated? I had to answer a very long list of hard questions with logic, not *"what ifs"* or *"maybes"* but what is. If you don't stop to ask yourself the tough questions, you will not learn the lessons, and if you don't learn the lessons, you will make the same mistakes repeatedly.

"If you pass the same tree twice in the woods, that means you are now lost."

—Author Unknown

Some people don't even know they are lost. They just keep going in the same circle repeatedly. The pain is there not to destroy you but to wake you up and get your attention that you are going in circles. Use the time of separation to find clarity in the smoke, instead of seeking another relationship without any growth from the last failed relationship. Reconciliation is also possible if both partners take the time to seek wisdom, acknowledge where they have fallen, and become much wiser individuals.

"One person's trash is another person's treasure."

Trash is trash, so stop using this quote to stay toxic. Jumping into another relationship without fixing your faults will have the same end as your previous relationship.

And no one pours new wine into old wineskins. Otherwise, the wine will burst the skins, and both the wine and the wineskins will be ruined. No, they pour new wine into new wineskins. (Mark 2:22 – NIV).

Take the time to learn, grow, and accept responsibility for where you went wrong. Even if the other person did all the damage, you still need to reflect and ask yourself what inside of you made you even attracted to that person in the first place. Why were you willing to tie yourself to this person? Why didn't you see the signs?

In examining so many divorces ever so often, it is the same story, but I often ask myself, *"If it is the same story, why is everyone making the same mistakes? She wants a divorce because her husband doesn't want to change. The husband wants a divorce because his wife has changed."* As Pastor Myles says, *"Love won't save your marriage, knowledge will."*

"How could he/she leave me? I thought he/she loved me!" Many have asked this question, but with knowledge, you can know how to avoid it. When this happened to me, I certainly had no intention of writing a book about it. When the Lord told me to write this book, I was not pleased. This ordeal was very embarrassing, yet the Lord wanted me to record it. I tried to sabotage the completion of this book several times.

The Lord told me that the people I hope never see this don't even read, so I shouldn't be too caught up in worrying about that. Secondly, it shouldn't matter if they do see it.

SEEKING MARRIAGE

But seek first the kingdom of God and His righteousness, and all these things shall be added to you. (Matthew 6:33 – NKJV).

Desiring to be married before even knowing your calling is risky. Imagine being called to the nations, but the person you married is comfortable spending the rest of his/her life in the same town they grew up in. You won't know your calling until you know the One who called you.

To men who keep saying, *"I need to find a wife to build with."* When God made Adam, it took a while before there was an Eve. Eve came into the picture after everything else was done and Adam was now lonely. You can be busy building yourself and going after your destiny, then when you get to a certain level of progress, the Lord brings a wife to you like He did for Adam. You can lose your purpose by marrying or dating someone uninterested in what God has called you to do.

As Solomon grew old, his wives turned his heart after other gods, and his heart was not fully devoted to the Lord his God, as the heart of David his father had been. (1 Kings 11:4 – NIV).

If Solomon's wives—as wise as he was—could turn him from God, then the wrong woman can do the same—or much worse—to you. Before you go seeking a wife, I encourage you to work on yourself and your relationship with the Lord so that when she does come along, the garden has already been built, and like a butterfly, she can enjoy it. Understand that, as a man, it does get very lonely and life will be hard regardless of your choices, but it is crucial that you make the choices that will make you feel accomplished.

I love to read about great men. I love to meet and speak with great men. It shows me that just being a man means life will be hard, but it can be worth it, if you work on yourself continually. Like the egg and the potato, the same boiling temperature water that hardens the egg softens the potato.

In seeking marriage, a woman should never marry a man who does not love her, and a man should never marry a woman who does not submit to him. If a *"wife"* at the altar tells the pastor to skip over the submission commitment, that should be the first sign to call the wedding off. If she does not see you fit to submit or lead, why go further? Too many men and women do not know when to walk away.

The one who does nothing but cause you pain will never be your peace. You may hesitate in walking away from the altar because you don't want to lose him or her, but you are just delaying the inevitable. If you are driving at 80mph and a car stops suddenly ahead, you don't sit back and hope your car stops or misses the car ahead, but you step on the brakes as hard as you can. If you don't step on that brake when you see the signs, you will leave that marriage dead or close to dead. By God's grace, this book is called *How I Lost My Wife to a Warlock*, not *How I Lost My Life to a Warlock*. Sometimes, to get the checkmate, you must sacrifice the queen. Sometimes, to win the war, you must lose the battle. You must kill the connection before the connection kills you. Irrational feelings will get you killed.

You may not agree with everything in this book, but that is okay. I am sure you may not agree with everything in the road code book, but you still follow all the rules because it is enforced for your safety. Every time you run a red light or refuse to stop at a stop sign, you run the risk of causing a serious accident. Imagine debating with a police officer about not wearing your seatbelt or helmet. He/she must write you a ticket for your own safety while you try to give him/her an excuse for why you were not wearing a seatbelt or a helmet.

Before you buy a house, car, or land, you will ask about its history because you don't want any surprises that might cost you in the future. I encourage you to do the same before you marry someone. You need to know what you are getting yourself into to decide if it will be worth it. Investigate the family tree, not to condemn anyone, but to know what you are getting yourself into. Marriage is very serious.

Suppose the family tree of the man you desire to marry has a record of men dying prematurely from non-communicable diseases because of poor eating habits. In that case, you will know that unless that man decides to eat healthily and take better care of himself, you will be a widow in a few years if you marry him. If the woman you want to marry has a past filled with promiscuity and bailing out on relationships when it gets hard, then you know unless she has worked on her character and made serious changes, she will do the same to you in a few years. Would you invest in a failing company? Then why gamble so recklessly with your life?

Let's say a woman marries a man at age twenty-five when her body is firm and there is no spot on her face in her prime concerning looks, then after fifteen years, she finds out that he is bisexual because he left her for another man. She just wasted fifteen years of her youth because an important question was not asked. For fifteen years, that issue was being suppressed and not dealt with and addressed fully.

Marriage is choosing to invest in someone, and you have a right to know what you are investing in. Someone came to me in 2022 asking for some advice concerning the difficulties he was facing while dating a young lady. He is a decent young man seeking a woman to call his own. He wanted to do the right thing. He seemed sad and told me the young lady wanted to put the relationship on pause because he was not *"handling her."*

"Is she a wild animal?" I asked.

I could deduce what her past was like and that she still had trauma dealing with. He confirmed that her ex was abusive to her, etc. I told him to call that a loss, focus on his business, and not tolerate the nonsense she was trying to bring into his life.

Six months later, she watched him on social media and realized he was making progress in his business. Then, she decided to reach out. He shot her down without hesitance. Whatever we tolerate, we won't change, so if he kept putting up with her to seek a relationship, it would have ended much worse for him. From the start, when he found out she had an abusive relationship, he should have pointed her to a therapist before even thinking about a relationship. A person's past can ruin your future. Always remember that.

I am not sure why men are demonized for not wanting to deal with certain types of women. I remember showing interest in a woman, thinking we could get to know each other a little better in a year or two. She made it very clear that she was not interested in that. She was looking for an older guy who was more stable, etc. Now, I didn't get enraged or try to justify anything. I didn't try to put her down for her preference. I went home and looked in the mirror, trying to see things from her point of view. She was seeking marriage in her thirties, and I didn't have that much to offer then. So, I encourage men to be okay with having a preference. As I continue to add value to myself and grow, I have become comfortable saying no to women I know are not God-sent. Now, if a woman sees that you are not operating at your full potential and decides to enter a relationship with you, she is taking a gamble believing she will win. It is on you to make her win.

I read a joke once that I think fits this context very well. A husband said to his wife, *"Honey, when I had no house or car, you were with me, but you were young, hot, and sexy. After years of marriage, I now have a house and cars. Maybe I should find a young, hot, sexy lady to be with now that you are getting old."*

His wife replied, *"You go date a 25-year-old hottie, and you'll be back to not having a house or cars after the divorce."*

Are you seeking a partner or a slave? Too often, when you ask someone what they are looking for in marriage, when they finish that list, you end up praying they never meet anyone you know. You feel sorry for whoever decides to marry them. Your spouse will never be able to make you feel one hundred percent fulfilled. It is not possible, and it is unfair. Don't try to place such a heavy burden on anyone.

I was watching an interview with a group of men and women, where they asked the women, *"Where do you think you can find a good man?"*

"Church," they replied.

"Do you ladies go to church?"

"No," was their reply with laughter.

I don't believe you can find decent men in church only, but if that is where they believe decent men are and don't go there, should I believe these women truly desire a good man? We see men searching for a good wife at the club, carnival, etc.

When I was younger, I believed the lie that if the gangsters in this country had the money, the crime would stop, but the reality is, the more money they make, the higher the crime rate would climb. Criminals exist, not because they lack resources, but when they start getting, they want more. That is how some people sound when they say, *"I just need a good man/woman."* Watch how toxic they get when that person walks into their lives. Just finding a good spouse will not make the marriage work. First, work on yourself to be a good spouse, then you can start seeking a good spouse.

AM I THE PRIZE?

A prize is not for everyone. If there are many others like you, how would that make you the prize? We live in a world that constantly tries to get everyone to be the same, yet somehow think they are special. You cannot follow the same trends, tattoos, hair, clothes, etc., and think you are the prize.

I encourage everyone to hold themselves to high standards and know their worth, but don't get your head so high in the clouds that you start lying to yourself. Some men walk around thinking, *"Oh, any woman would be lucky to have me because I don't cheat."* You may not cheat, but you are very disrespectful and verbally abusive. Refrain from ticking your check box and concluding that you are the prize. Some women who go around thinking, *"I am the prize"* often think they are because they have their own home, degree, and money. Yes, these are outstanding achievements, making you a prize to your family. Your nieces and nephews will love you for the many benefits you worked so hard for, but this won't make you a prize to a man who is not looking for a handout. You become the prize when you seek marriage with the mindset of serving the one God has for you. Step off the pedestal and get off the high horse so you can look into your spouse's eyes instead of looking down on them.

You can study the course for the job you desire, but you would never get a degree in English if your goal is to be a Spanish teacher. Likewise, if a successful marriage is your goal, then it is best to study what is required.

When I think about the wife I desire, I also think of what will be required of me to cultivate her/improve her life. I would love to say,

"Well, she should just accept and love me for me," but I know this is not how it works. Those unwilling to change and follow wise advice will keep hoping and complaining instead of following the rules. Seek marriage with humility and not your ego.

MEN SEEKING MARRIAGE

For the men seeking to get married, this is one of the most important decisions you will ever make in your life. Please do not make this decision in haste or on emotions only. MMA fighter, McGregor, told the world that he is the man he is today because of the woman by his side. Like many other great men who reached great heights, they tell you the importance of having the right woman beside you.

I have met many married men, stuck in a job they hate, in debt, in a sexless marriage, their wives don't respect them, and their children don't listen to them. If you think it can't get any worse, it can and will if the man does not wake up. In seeking marriage, you are seeking a helper who doesn't just help around the house but can help you take care of the assignments you carry. This is not someone you will think less of because only someone equal to or higher than you can help you. Your helper will make up for what you lack. You are in the driver's seat, but she is next to you, holding a map. You might be an extrovert, but she is an introvert. You might know how to make a lot of money, but she knows how to save it or help you spend it wisely. A help-meet is not a slave. The woman you marry is far from being a slave. On the wedding day, the man stands at the altar while the woman is taken to the altar by her father and given to the man because the husband now takes over from her father. It is now his job to take care of her in every way. His role is to protect, provide, etc.

Sex before marriage will complicate your decision-making and cloud your judgment. Sad to say, many have gotten married because the woman *"put it down"* on them so well. If you should take the sex away, the woman had nothing to offer except her body. Her body will not raise your children, but her character and values will. Seek and you will find. Stop believing the lies that no good women are left.

Do not give your strength to women, nor your ways to that which destroys kings. (Proverbs 31:3 – NKJV).

This scripture warns men not to give away their strength—time, resources, etc.—to women. Some men get tricked, played, or conned on payday. That is when they take their resources and give to a woman for one reason or another. I have heard old men confess that they wasted their earnings when they were younger, spending recklessly on pretty women. Some men are willing to give away their strength until none is left, making them weak men. I have seen countless men use all their resources to send a woman to college to get degrees, etc. After graduation, the woman tells them to get lost.

Andre Bloomfield was charged with the murder of Shanteel Whyte, his alleged girlfriend, whom he killed in 2020. This shocked the island of Jamaica. It is alleged that after he invested his resources in this young lady, helping to build a house, etc., the young lady wanted out of the relationship, leading to Andre killing Miss Whyte. Your resources are for your family, to take care of your wife and children and to secure their future, not to be spent foolishly on women.

Ask yourself, *"If I was that woman, would I marry me?"*

A king can marry the maid, but the queen will never marry the gardener.

I love going close to a group of women with my ears open, just listening to their conversations with a notebook out. Women, especially younger women, enjoy talking about their spouse's accomplishments. Older women will talk more about what their spouse is up to, the places they visit, etc. Young men speak about the beauty and shape of the woman they have, and older men will speak more about how much their woman takes good care of them. They will brag about her cooking, etc.

WOMEN DESIRING MARRIAGE

Many years ago, a woman proposing to a man would be considered taboo, but now it is becoming normal. A wife is someone to be found and persuaded by a man to become his. It is not a woman's place to try and change a man, so if his beliefs and morals do not seem right, then please don't believe marrying him means he will one day change. Tell him to go and transform his mindset and come back. If he values you at all, he will do so. If you marry a man who doesn't value you, he will not value your ideas or feelings. If you marry a murderer/drug dealer, convincing yourself that you can change him is not wise. Marry a man who knows his purpose. If he knows his purpose, he knows where he is going, and you can help him get there. Being a wife means being a helper, and you are wired to help. If he doesn't know his purpose, then he doesn't know where he is going, and if he doesn't know where he is going, you will not have a purpose in that marriage. So many married women are bored because it has been the same for years.

When the husband is not going anywhere new, it can lead to affairs being birth from boredom. You are partnering with a man to fulfill a purpose/calling. Marrying a man with just potential will feel unnatural because you feel like you are telling a man how to be a man. Many women have contacted me, asking me to speak to their spouses to help them. I can't forget a businesswoman who told me she would pay her husband's mentorship fee if I accepted him into the program. I had to decline because she would only waste her money and my time. This man was very unwilling to do anything that would require growth in his life. He even said he didn't need help. She married a man with potential, but he had no intention of trying to reach his full potential.

As a woman, if you can reflect on your life, you will see that, at some point, you have been used for one reason or another. The problem is that some women allow the wrong person to use them. Next to every successful man is a woman. It could be a wife, mom, sister or daughter. A woman is the only one designed to take what is given to her and multiply it.

When King Jesus needed to enter this world, the Lord God, who made us all, still needed to find a woman He could use to enter this realm. The criminal network becomes stronger when they find women they can use because they know the power of a woman. A woman is like fertile land, willing to give you whatever you plant in abundance. I am very aware that some women will see this and still feel uncomfortable about being used but will still go to work to be used by a boss/company who doesn't love them. Allow the man who loves and cherishes you to use you for the betterment of the family. So many cringe at this because they imagine being a doormat, but that is far from the truth.

An excellent wife is the crown of her husband, but she who brings shame is like rottenness in his bones. (Proverbs 12:4 – ESV).

Wishful thinking is your enemy because it makes you believe the lie you tell yourself. I have a hard time sometimes getting through to women because it is like walking on eggshells to try and get the point across without hurting their feelings. After all, once emotions get involved, logic goes out the window.

I remember telling a young lady she had to go out for men to see her, if she desired to get married, but her wishful thinking was that a man would break into her house and ask her to marry him. Wishful thinking is that the man with no intention of changing will change. I have seen wishful thinking turn into witchcraft. A few women who do not match what a man is looking for long-term take it upon themselves to use charms or visit mediums to cast spells for the man to stay with them.

I watched a group of people do an amazing experiment where five women entered a room and discussed who would be the first choice for a man seeking a mate. They decided this with wishful thinking and emotions, trying not to hurt anyone's feelings instead of being honest. Then five men walked into the room giving honest opinions on who was their first choice and rearranged everything. The lady they voted for as the first choice was moved to the back of the line. They hyped this lady up and told her being loud and aggressive is what men are looking for and that they loved her personality. Well, she found out a few hours later that it was a lie. The woman they all overlooked because of her feminine presence ended up being the first choice for all five men who were in the room.

Imagine leaving your house with bad breath, and your friends smell it but say nothing. They don't want to hurt your feelings, so they allow you to go through the day without knowing the truth. You just need one friend who can look you in the eye and tell you that you have bad breath. The truth will cause you to pause and maybe get some breath mints or brush your teeth. But, way too often, that one friend is labeled as a hater. To be honest, sometimes your haters will be more honest than many who say they love you.

I remember visiting a well-known church in my country, and the topic was *"Marriage."* After about two hours of questions, not one man stood up to ask a question or share his opinion. The women wasted no time speaking their minds or asking questions, but so many men have gotten accustomed to suffering in quiet desperation that they don't even want to share opinions or ask questions on the topic of marriage. You can't desire something and speak down on it at the same time. You want marriage, but every time you get the chance to speak about it, you say you don't need it. That ego will rob you every time. If you honestly don't want to get married or have children, that is okay. We see people do this and are living decent lives, so hats off to them. But if deep in your heart you want to get married, you want children, you want a family, then do not speak down on marriage because belittling your heart's desire will only take it further away from you.

"A young heart desires money but an old heart desires family."
—Author Unknown

VICTIM MINDSET

An experiment was conducted in which five women were informed that makeup would be applied to create scars on their faces. Subsequently, these women proceeded to another room for a job interview. Upon their return, those who were not selected for the position expressed the belief that their rejection was due to the perceived scars. To dispel this misconception, mirrors were given to the rejected women, revealing that their faces did not actually have any scars. The experiment involved informing them beforehand about the makeup application to assess the impact on their perceptions.

Society tries to force women into believing their scars dictate how they should be treated. There are beautiful black women who believe they are less than other races because of the psychological scars they had gotten in this world. When you no longer think like a victim, you will see yourself as much more and act accordingly. Being a victim is not a flex but a mindset used to justify bad behavior and to avoid taking responsibility so you can feel justified for the wrong you did. Your trauma is not an excuse to treat your spouse badly.

"I had an affair because Tommy made me feel bad and I was hurt" is a victim mindset. Any man or woman who sees themselves as a victim will not take responsibility for any wrongdoing.

I DO OR WELL DONE?

If you desire to hear *"I do"* more than *"Well done, My faithful servant,"* then you are in trouble, my friend. Do not throw the Blueprint God gave you away just because you want to get married.

Don't have sex before marriage, hoping the man will propose, and don't give up your authority as head, hoping the woman will accept your proposal.

Everyone carries an assignment we should protect, and your marriage should support your call, not deport it.

CHAPTER 31

The Snake is Now a Dragon

The book of Genesis describes a snake in the garden, but the book of Revelation talks about a dragon.

When you fail to kill the snake, you will one day face a dragon, which will be much harder to kill. There was a snake in my marriage for years. He whispered lies in both our ears and fed off our confusion and rage. A very small disagreement could one day become a big obstacle. Don't underestimate the patience of the snake because he will size you up before he strikes. Imagine him feeding off the petty arguments until they become fights, and the more he eats, the bigger he gets. Imagine the fights and disagreements over a six-year period and how much he has grown in that time frame.

In your anger do not sin: Do not let the sun go down while you are still angry, and do not give the devil a foothold. (Ephesians 4:26-27 – NIV).

The Blueprint warns us not to give the devil a foothold. So many married couples go to bed angry at each other with their backs turned, or one sleeps in another room, not realizing the snake gets a little stronger every time this happens. It starts with turning your back to your spouse in bed, then sleeping in another room, until it moves to staying out late, and then sleeping somewhere else. Resentment is the killer of love.

Always address and settle conflicts with wisdom; being ready to forgive is how you starve the snake. How will you handle the dragon if you struggle with the snake? The dragon's skin is like armor. He breathes fire. He has wings, and he is no longer on his belly but on his feet.

SIGNS THE SNAKE IS NOW A DRAGON IN YOUR MARRIAGE

The thief comes only to steal and kill and destroy; I have come that they may have life, and have it to the full. (John 10:10 - NIV).

STEAL

The enemy comes to the marriage to steal something, and if you pay attention, you will see the main things he has come to steal. He has come for the main tools that make a marriage work. He will steal money from the marriage because he knows the lack of money in a marriage leads to arguments and builds frustration. He will cause broken pipes, car trouble, every and any way to cause spending. He will take advantage of poor money management until the family has sleepless nights from being one paycheck away from being homeless. He knows that women cannot function properly when no money is in the house because women think a lot when they don't feel secure. So, stealing the money will ultimately steal the sex because the last thing a woman wants is you being on top of her when the light and water are about to get disconnected, and there is no food on the table.

While the man can have sex, even if the world ends tomorrow, it is not so for most women. So, when sex is gone, the man becomes frustrated, and if both partners are not mature and know how to communicate these important matters, things will go downhill.

Sex and money are not really discussed in most churches. If the devil can't steal your money because you handle it well, he tries to steal your health. Recently, I got a sad phone call when a friend told me his sister's husband died. *"Why now?"* he said, *"My sister finally got a good man in her life. They got approved for another loan to get another house. Business was looking good. My sister loves him, and he takes care of his family. This isn't fair."* I know too many married men who are not well in their bodies and have no use for their wives in bed.

KILL

The enemy comes to kill, so always remember that he is not to be ignored. If the marriage is dead, who killed it? Did the autopsy reveal the cause of death? Time of death? The enemy is so sneaky that he can kill your marriage long before you even realize it is dead. I see dead marriages often, but the couples have not noticed that it is dead because it has not started to smell yet. As it deteriorates, they will ask, *"What is that smell?"*

The enemy comes to kill the passion and romance. Without passion, it starts to feel like a burden to do the work in the marriage. The enemy will try to kill the woman's womb, knowing it can help break the marriage. This attack will cause frustration and doubt. He will attempt to kill anything he finds with life in that house, even innocent children. He comes with sickness, bad habits, and many other weapons.

I remember in 2022, the Lord showed me the plans of a snake to kill a man who was just stepping into greatness. Venturing out into business and life was looking good. He had a good woman and a baby girl to care for, so the snake sought to take him. The man started having very strange dreams of being killed, and I would tell him the spirit of death was after him and that he should pray.

Then I had a dream that he was in a car, and I saw the car driving over a grave. When I woke up, I understood the enemy wanted to kill him in a car crash. The Lord sent me to his house to pray for him. I thank God he is still here with his family today to continue being a good man in his house. When the enemy comes to kill, his target will first be the man—in most cases—because it gets a little easier to destroy the family.

DESTROY

After the enemy has stolen and killed, he has now destroyed the marriage. It is burnt to ashes, and he hovers over it, breathing fire. If there is any hope of defeating this dragon at this stage, you need to have on the whole armor of God. Don't be passive with this snake. Don't keep him as a pet. I remember reading a story about a lady who had a pet python. The snake slept beside her every night, and one day, the snake stopped eating. After a few days, she took the snake to the vet to find out if it was sick. The veterinarian told her the snake was not eating because it had been sizing her up and making room to be able to swallow her.

ONLY THROUGH OBEDIENCE CAN WE WIN

The same way the snake deceived Eve in the garden by convincing her to ignore the rules, is the same thing he is doing today. He encourages everyone to do whatever they want, ignore structure, and do what pleases them. He influences you to obey your feelings instead of obeying the Architect who made it all.

Imagine if the coach's advice to his soccer team going out to play was, *"Just do whatever makes you happy out there. Goalkeeper, you can play attack. My number one striker can be the goalkeeper."* Would it be possible for that team to win with such confusion? So why do you think ignoring the strategic instructions in the Blueprint because of how you feel about it will give you the win?

This snake has been on this earth long before you. The only way to win is to listen to the One far older and wiser than that serpent. Are the rules easy to follow? No, but when the consequences that come from breaking the rules start to happen, you realize the rules are not worth breaking. The Blueprint tells us that sex comes after marriage, but society, influenced by the snake, says it is okay to have sex before marriage, but there is no mention of the trauma and baggage that come from doing so. Imagine how much better our lives would be if we waited for the husband/wife before we took such a step.

Today, people go to the altar for marriage, looking like they just returned from World War 2. They are emotionally damaged with much trauma and demons attached, then blame marriage when it feels like a living hell. The snake never changes its tactics because it works. Likewise, the Word of the Lord works, and He has not changed. The world continues to lose its grip on reality because they are buying into the lies. If you are not willing to follow the blueprint of marriage, then my advice is to save yourself the trouble. It is not a sin to be unmarried.

Now to the unmarried and the widows I say: It is good for them to stay unmarried, as I do. But if they cannot control themselves, they should marry, for it is better to marry than to burn with passion. (1 Corinthians 7:8-9 – NIV).

If you are unwilling to do what it takes to make your marriage work, then there is no shame in not getting into a marriage. You decide the actions, not the reaction. If you decide to neglect the Blueprint given to make the marriage work, you have no control over the consequences that come with that. When building a house, you follow the code given that it can pass the inspection when it is done. You need the correct material to build the house we call marriage. After ten years of marriage, so many are stuck at the foundation level because they lack the material to go any higher, and the embarrassment of divorce comes in. Jesus said, **"For which of you, intending to build a tower, does not sit down first and count the cost, whether he has enough to finish it—" (Luke 14:28 – NKJV).** You can put so much planning into a wedding with zero plans for the marriage. You can know the exact cost for the wedding, but the marriage you blindly walk into. Please understand that dating someone for ten years and being married for ten years is not the same. This is why we see couples date for years and then get a divorce after marriage. The material needed is not the same.

"Cutting out a man's tongue does not prove he is a liar but shows he has much to say and that you are afraid of hearing it."
—*Author Unknown.*

Society tries its best to silence anyone who speaks the truth. The Pharisees murdering Stephen for telling the truth seemed barbaric, but is it any different today? Yet, even while Steven was being stoned to death with his last breath, he said, *"Lord, lay not this sin to their charge."* In other words, Lord, don't punish them for this great sin they are committing.

Above all, have fervent and unfailing love for one another, because love covers a multitude of sins [it overlooks unkindness and unselfishly seeks the best for others]. (1 Peter 4:8 - AMP).

After six years of being in a struggling marriage, always in debt, and owing months of rent, I was unable to accomplish something as simple as getting a driver's license. I told God I was ready to do what He called me to. I prayed, *"Lord, I do understand that I will not be at the house anymore, but help give me the strength to take care of my family."*

In a few months, the six months' rent owed was paid off, the water bill paid off, I got my driver's license, started a mentorship program, and the list goes on. I stop by the house every two weeks to take out the trash, take everyone to the beach or park to do an activity, and then I leave. When it is time to tell my boys goodbye, I can't help but wonder what it would be like if we had just done things right.

Anyone who does not provide for their relatives, and especially for their own household, has denied the faith and is worse than an unbeliever. (1 Timothy 5:8 – NIV).

Separation or divorce is not a reason to stop taking care of your family. I have not held my hand back in doing that, even though I have had moments where I wrestled with it. I have had thoughts of pulling my hands away, but the fear of the Lord and the stubborn love I have would not allow me to do it. What I considered to be a weakness holding me back was the very same thing God loved about me because in my weakness, He flexes His muscles and makes me strong.

I would look in the mirror and tell myself how much I despise the fact that I can't hate those who have done me wrong. I dislike the fact that I was praying for someone who caused me shame and pain.

About two years into marriage, when my ex-wife was pregnant with my first son, we went to the hospital for a check-up, and a nurse called us aside to have a word with us. She was a servant of God with a word for us. She started to prophesy the good things the Lord had in store for us. Then she said to my wife at the time, *"Don't miss out on what the Lord has in store for your husband. Help him to get the houses and cars."* The nurse was having a woman-to-woman talk with my ex-wife, so I stepped back a little, but I was able to hear a part of the conversation. The nurse told her that if she became a hindrance, God would remove her from the picture. Five years later, it was so.

The story of Joseph is one of my favorite stories to read. He was sold out and betrayed by his brothers, but he didn't allow hatred to consume him to get revenge.

Then Joseph said to his brothers, "Come close to me." When they had done so, he said, "I am your brother Joseph, the one you sold into Egypt! And now, do not be distressed and do not be angry with yourselves for selling me here, because it was to save lives that God sent me ahead of you. For two years now there has been famine in the land, and for the next five years there will be no plowing and reaping. But God sent me ahead of you to preserve for you a remnant on earth and to save your lives by a great deliverance. So then, it was not you who sent me

here, but God. He made me father to Pharaoh, lord of his entire household and ruler of all Egypt." (Genesis 45:4-8 - NIV).

Sometimes you must leave the people you love to preserve life. A man left his sick child at home to go search for Jesus so that he could request Him to heal his child. If he had stayed by the child's side, that child would have died.

May this failed marriage of mine be the marriage that saves, strengthens, start, and preserves yours.

CHAPTER 32

Prayer Points

The Lord revealed to me that some men have been bewitched and stolen from their families. As the practice of witchcraft increases, especially in America, more people are falling victim.

A believer who was in witchcraft and sex magic many years ago also told me how she used witchcraft to get a pastor to fall for her, and that she was only able to do that because the pastor was already backsliding.

He who digs a pit will fall into it, and whoever breaks through a wall will be bitten by a serpent. (Ecclesiastes 10:8 – NKJV).

Getting out of the will of God already puts you in a vulnerable place to be bewitched. If your spouse is determined not to walk as the Lord commands and ignores the signs and warnings, you can't force that person to do otherwise. We tend to stumble at times, and these prayer points should help you cover your spouse.

These prayer points can be used, even if you are not yet married. Pray for your spouse, even if you have not met them yet.

Therefore this is what the Sovereign LORD says: I am against your magic charms with which you ensnare people like birds and I will tear them from your arms; I will set free the people that you ensnare like birds. (Ezekiel 13:20 – NIV).

Father, in the name of Jesus Christ, I come against every magic charm being used to manipulate and control (insert name). I rebuke any wicked spirit that is claiming (insert name) in the sea. Let the fire of God destroy every black pot and incantation. Every wicked device of the enemy is neutralized now in Jesus Christ's mighty name.

It is written in Job 5:12, He frustrates the devices of the crafty, so that their hands cannot carry out their plans. I declare and decree that every charm, every black pot, every spell, every device of the witches and warlocks are neutralized now in Jesus Christ's mighty name. Psalm 121:7 declares, The LORD will keep you from all harm— he will watch over your life; Lord keep (insert name) from all evil and watch over (insert name) life going out and coming in. Keep (insert name) from all traps and scheme of darkness. I come boldly to Your throne of grace to obtain mercy on behalf of (insert name). According to Hebrews 4:16, we come boldly unto the throne of grace, that we may obtain mercy, and find grace to help in time of need. Have mercy on (insert name), mighty God.

Hide me from the conspiracy of the wicked, from the plots of evildoers. (Psalm 64:2 – NIV).

Father, I pray even now that, in the mighty name of our Lord Jesus Christ, You hide (insert name) from the secret counsel of the wicked. When they search for (insert name), they won't find (insert name) because (insert name) is hidden in You. When they call (insert name) name, they won't find (insert name). When they look for (insert name), they will not find (insert name). Your Word says in Jeremiah 15:21, "I will deliver you from the power of the wicked. I will set you free from the clutches of violent people." Deliver (insert name) from the hands of the witches and warlocks. Free (insert name) from manipulations of darkness, and deliver (insert name) mind from webs of trickery and deceit. Every arrow of lust, perversion, adultery, fornication, or sexual immorality of any kind shot against (insert name), I bind you in Jesus' name, and I pull you down. I pull down any thoughts that desire to overrule the knowledge of God according to 2 Corinthians 10:5. We demolish arguments and every pretension that sets itself up against the knowledge of God, and we take captive every thought to make it obedient to Christ. I cover (insert name) mind from attacks of depression and anxiety in Jesus Christ's mighty Name. Help (insert name) to submit fully to You, mighty God, so that (insert name) can walk out the word that says in James 4:7, "Submit to God. Resist the devil and he will from you."

I pray (insert name) will be alert and sober-minded, for Your Word says in 1 Peter 5:8-9 that, like a roaring lion, the devil goes around seeking who he may devour. I pray (insert name) be vigilant, spiritually awake and sensitive to what is happening around his/her surroundings. 1 Corinthians 10:13 declares, No temptation is new to us but God is faithful and will not allow us to be tempted more than we can handle, and He will provide a way out that we can endure it. I pray that (insert name) will not fall victim to these temptations. Faithful God, be a shield for (insert name) and keep (insert name) from all arrows of temptation. Lead (insert name) from temptation and deliver (insert name) from evil. Arise, mighty God, and let your enemies be scattered. Let those who seek to destroy (insert names) be brought into confusion, and let the angel of the Lord chase them through dark and slippery places. Psalm 17:13 declares, Arise, O Lord, disappoint them, cast them down, deliver our souls from the wicked. Free this marriage from any wicked web that the enemy has entangled us in.

I will destroy the cities of your land and tear down all your strongholds. I will destroy your witchcraft and you will no longer cast spells. (Micah 5:11-12 – NIV).

Mighty God, by the authority You have given me, I pull down and demolish every wicked word spoken against my marriage. I declare and decree that no power of witchcraft shall manifest in my marriage. It is written, "What therefore God hath joined together, let not man put asunder." (Matthew 19:6). I declare that no man can pull us apart, no witch, no wizard, no power of darkness can pull apart what God has put together. I command every blockage and barrier erected against this marriage to fall. Make our thoughts clear, mighty God. Psalm 71:1 declares, In thee, O Lord, do I put my trust: let me never be put to confusion. Let every spell of confusion sent against this marriage fall to the ground. Deliver my household from the wicked intentions and plans of the enemy. Psalms 59:2 declares, Deliver me from the workers of the iniquity. Psalm 144:6 declares, Cast forth lightning and scatter them: shoot out Thine arrows and destroy them. Scatter every demon on assignment against this marriage. Scatter their plans, and destroy their altars in Jesus' mighty name. Psalms 20:8 declares, They are brought down and fallen but we are risen and stand upright. The works of darkness have fallen but we stand firm on the rock, our Lord and Savior. Romans 10:13 says, Whosoever shall call upon the name of the Lord shall be saved. (Call on Jesus). Deliver us from our enemies, and rescue us from the wicked plots of the workers of darkness. Amen.

About the Author

Trey Walters is the Founder of Breaking Strongholds Ministries, father of two, kingdom entrepreneur, mentor, life coach, and writer. As a man on a mission, he uses his prophetic and teaching gifts to advance the kingdom of heaven on earth with biblical principles to help couples build successful marriages.

In 2019, Trey started to experience the most difficult time in his life: drowning in debt, constant hospital visits with one of his sons, who had an unexplainable illness, and his other son, who had an awful speech impediment. At this very low place in life, his wife had an affair with a warlock who had one goal, and that was to take them all out. During this time, God taught him warfare strategies to regain his life and happiness. He was able to rise above these trials to become a man of value.

www.ingramcontent.com/pod-product-compliance
Lightning Source LLC
Chambersburg PA
CBHW060526090426
42735CB00011B/2385